Passport TO THE World

Looking Back While Moving On

LINDA KLEIN MEANS

outskirts
press

For Jim—supportive always

For Liz—my rock and best friend

For Ella, Maya and Lana

my three beautiful granddaughters

TABLE OF CONTENTS

Chapter 1

---~~~---

AMAZING GRACE

ANTOINETTE RAYNOR—THE NAME can still evoke feelings of embarrassment, shame, curiosity, even a little jealousy. After all, what was she doing with a name so exotic in our little world of Karens, Lindas, Loises, Patricias, Anns? One local mother who had theatrical ambitions for her children even before they were born, had named her daughter Dawn Rae; even that was straying too far from the norm in the opinion of some. I grew up in a small town in rural Illinois in the 1950's, not New York City.

In addition to the name, there was the matter of her hair, a wild, unkempt black mane, so unlike our prim, carefully trimmed little brown or blonde dos. We were fifth-grade mini-versions of Debbie Reynolds or Doris Day. In 6th grade, she was already a full-blown Anna Magnani, the Italian sexpot of the movies of the day. Anna Magnani portrayed prostitutes and other social outcasts; I don't mean that Antoinette was acting out in any such way, but that seemed to be the image she evoked in our straight-laced little town.

I think we knew instinctively that our parents wouldn't approve of Antoinette. Debbie Reynolds and Doris Day were screen images of what our parents wanted us to be. Bosomy, sex-appeal-exuding Anna Magnani, (minus the fame, stardom and money) was everything we were NOT supposed to be. Remember, this was the fifties; the pill had not been invented. We were pre-pubescent, but not by much. The surest way a young girl could ruin herself and her family was to get pregnant, or even to get a reputation for being "wild." Associating with someone like Antoinette could only mean trouble. We were farmers, always just one bad season away from bankruptcy. We had troubles enough.

And her clothes, good grief, where did she get those clothes? From the ragbag, was our guess, and on top of that they were none too clean. The rest of us weren't quite the fashion plates we thought ourselves to be. Our clothes were made by our mothers or purchased from some place like Penny's, before it went all upscale—but they were clean, they fit properly, they were so skillfully mended that only the wearer and her mother knew they were mended. And we had coats, leggings and mittens for the winter, sundresses for the summer, Sunday Best dresses for church.

Antoinette appeared to have none of that. Did she even have a mother? I suppose so, although I don't remember ever seeing one, but then, they didn't stay in town long, or rather on the farm near town where her father worked as a day laborer. Ah yes, her father—"Dirty Raynor," I heard the other men call him behind his back. They were all hard-working men who wore work clothes, but the same overworked women who kept their children in adequate wardrobes and states of personal hygiene did the same for their husbands. Aparently no one was doing that for Dirty Raynor. I never did learn his first name. Years later I learned from my brother that there was indeed a mother. In financial desperation she had hired herself out as a housekeeper to someone my brother described as having "the worst reputation of anyone in town."

I can only imagine what daily life with such a man was like, but it seemed to leave little time for minding and nurturing the kids, of which there were many, never mind sewing, cooking, overseeing bathtime, etc. I've since asked around among a few friends from those days, and no one even remembered her existence, that's how invisible she was. Except my younger brother, who had to sit next to her younger sister Geraldine, in a set-up his teacher was trying out that year--you were placed immediately next to another child for the year, in the hope that you would become "partners" and "friends."

"Oh yes, I remember them," he said. "Our teacher seated us two by two for the entire year. I got Geraldine and she peed her pants every single day." Funny, yes, but also heart-breaking--how much trauma has a fourth-grader undergone if she is wetting her pants in school every single day?

It didn't occur to me or anyone in my little clique of fifth grade girls that being a newcomer in such a place couldn't have been easy. We were girls who had known each other since birth, girls whose parents, grandparents, great-grandparents and beyond had farmed next to each other on land they inherited, or partially inherited, for four, five, sometimes six generations (some were preceded on the land only by native Americans). We didn't think about the fact that no one looked after Antoinette, took care of her, defended her. We just knew she was different, and not in a good way.

Our cruelties seem small by today's standards, but I'm sure she remembers them still, as I do. I remember nothing overt. We didn't wait in ambush for her, or call her names, or engage in any kind of physical or even emotional abuse, not consciously anyway. We simply included her in nothing, not even the right to sit with us at lunch. She always ate alone. She was never invited to parties. And of course we laughed about her clothes; not to her face, we were too well brought up for that, but she knew. Since we did "nothing," I don't think it occurred to any of us that we were being mean. That was the problem with her "invisibility"--she wasn't really invisible, she was right there in front of me--and her clothes and hair, if nothing else, drew attention. No, it was more a matter of my blindness; nothing and no one like her was part of our known world, so I just didn't see her--I saw the coat, but not the person beneath. On the loneliest day of my life, I was probably never as lonely as Antoinette was all the time.

One day, one of the first really chilly days of fall, Antoinette outdid even her own bizarre daily "fashion" show by appearing in a coat so big, so threadbare, so ragged, so dirty, so ugly that I remember it still as the worst coat I have ever seen. None of our parents would have allowed us to leave the house in such a thing. Had it been a cast-off of her grand-mother's? Did girls like Antoinette have grandmothers? Its wearer must have felt even more shrouded by shame than by the coat itself.

I didn't notice it at the time--Antoinette was one of those I have since come to think of as "the invisible ones"--but she had arrived at school already on the defensive, loaded for bear. She knew she was an outcast, and she knew the coat would eventually attract the most negative and humiliating kind of attention

As it happened, I was standing with my gang of girlfriends before school began that day, laughing and talking, not about the coat, we hadn't even noticed it yet, but Antoinette thought otherwise. Suddenly she came racing at us, eyes blazing, nails bared like claws.

"You're all a bunch of cats!" she screamed. "And I hate every one of you!"

Antoinette herself did look like a cat. Not a tame little pussycat playing with a ball of pink yarn, like the rest of us, but a wild, feral cat, in fear of her life, fearless in attack because she had nothing to lose anyway. In her wild abandon she was more like a leopard than a housecat--but she was in fact so powerless that the crowd around her barely noticed, other than to note that she was even crazier than we thought. Why did she wear that coat? Probably because she had two choices--wear it or freeze.

To take the one tiny bit of credit I can claim, I didn't laugh at her as some others did, but I didn't defend her either, and I thought the whole scene was pretty funny.

The after dinner routine at our house was that my mother washed the dinner dishes while I simultaneously dried and regaled her with the events of the day. Of course, Antoinette and her coat and her fit was the big story of that day. I included scintillating details about just how awful, how huge, how dirty, how utterly ridiculous the coat was. The color, if you could call it that, was some sort of grayish, brownish, greenish, blackish dirt color, no longer even recognizable as a color. I didn't know any homeless people then, but later in life, when I began encountering them, their coats, colorlessness and shapelessness and hopelessness and all, reminded me of Antoinette's.

My mother listened in silence, then said, without looking at me, "Oh, that poor girl. I just hope you didn't take part in any of that."

Suddenly my story was funny no longer.

Shame engulfed me, as it does to this day when I think of it. The Raynors left town soon after, to where I have no idea. Antoinette, with her flashing eyes, courageous temper, and wild black hair, was beautiful even then, in a way that we homogeneous fifth graders couldn't begin to comprehend. Had we secretly envied her wildness, her freedom from the strict rules that imprisoned us? How could I have been so blind to her pain?

Her courage in the face of her powerlessness and her invisibility to the rest of us makes me think, now, of other "invisibles" of that time--Tedine, for example.

Tedine was the only black girl in our little white school. I never heard the N word or any other racial slur used against her. I always smiled at her when I saw her in the hallway, and she always smiled back. And in that tiny little school, that was the sum total of our contact with each other, and of the time I spent thinking about her. I never met her parents, never knew where she lived, never saw her at a party, or even at lunch. Perhaps she went home, wherever that might have been. There was a little section called "Old Town," consisting of a few very modest houses, at the end of our little town (pop. 755 at that time) where our few black families lived. Tedine surely lived there--where else? but why did I never wonder which house? We all knew where everybody lived. And why did I never see a single other resident of "Old Town" anywhere else? Not shopping in our little town's only grocery store--not anywhere.

And it wasn't an issue of clothes--Tedine was always immaculately and neatly dressed in clothes similar to what the rest of us wore. I think she was trying to be invisible, with help from the family that obviously cared for her, took care of her, tried to keep her safe--but the color of her skin wouldn't allow that. Again, she was always right there in front of me, perfectly visible--if I hadn't been blind.

She became "visible" to me only during my senior year, when our English teacher chose a few essays to be read aloud in class, including one by Tedine. I remember only the first line, "It hasn't been easy, being the only black person in this school..." Again, I was flooded with shame, so much so that I didn't hear the rest. She had been amongst us all those years, even more visible than any of the rest of us because of her skin color, and I had never once bothered to really even take note of her existence. I can only remember her gliding silently, gracefully through the halls, always perfectly dressed and groomed, always smiling, although now I remember the sadness behind the smile. And it was the end of her senior year. Too late now. And there was the boy with learning disabilities who we all thought was "dumb".....waking up. opening your eyes, learning to see is painful--because you are then forced to see yourself and all your deficits.

I wish I could meet the women Antoinette and Tedine grew up to be, get to know them at last. Antoinette broke out with a wild scream and was at least invisible no more. Tedine spoke up quietly, at last, and to me at least, was invisible no more. Both are with me still, and always will be, along with so many others who would once have passed right in front of me without being seen.

I suspect that the Raynors had lived in many little towns as featureless (to them) as ours, and were to live in many more before Antoinette graduated, if she ever did. I doubt she remembers any of them, individually, or us, as well as I remember her. Her ancestors were not buried in any of those towns. She did not have a great-aunt or a grandparent on every street corner, noting her every move and casually mentioning them all to her parents. And Tedine? She had family, I know, but none were ever seen except Tedine, during school hours--and we didn't see her.

I loved my extended family, but I sometimes found that surplus of relatives annoying. Privacy as a concept just didn't exist. But perhaps Antoinette and Tedine envied the sense of safety, security and belonging to a network of people who actually cared about our well-being that all this caregiving (or snooping, as I sometimes thought of it) engendered.

On Thanksgiving day at our homes, our mothers got up at 5 AM to put the 25 pound turkey in the oven. Aunts, uncles, cousins and grandparents would arrive before noon, laden with salads, vegetables, pies, breads. At Christmastime, a tree went up. Presents were few and modest (sometimes things like "practical" brown underwear from a grandmother, "treasures" from Aunt Carrie's attic), but all the trappings of Christmas, including the Christmas eve service, the big family dinner the next day, were there. I don't think those things were happening at Antoinette's house. Were they at Tedine's? I have no idea.

Invisibility happens to millions of people, everywhere. I've felt invisible myself at times. We tend not to notice or think about them until one, or a group, breaks out--either wildly and violently or quietly, with eloquent words. But I think few people remain invisible forever. They break out, perhaps violently, or they speak out, perhaps with a Nobel-prize-winning poem, or they simply die inside. Blindness happens to lots of us too--even if our opthomologist tells us we have 20/20 vision.

Maybe they are part of the reason why I have always so loved the old hymn by former slave trader John Newton, whose long slow spiritual awakening eventually lead him to study Christian theology, become an ardent abolitionist, and eventually be instrumental in the abolishment of slavery in Britain. He wrote it for his New Year's Day sermon in 1773; the Slave Trade Act, abolishing slavery, was passed in 1807.

You all know the words to that great old hymn--....."I once was lost but now am found, was blind but now I see."

Chapter 2

THE BLUES FOR MY BLUE BOY

I WAS 11 years old, and standing at the front door, where I'd been most of the morning, anxiously awaiting the arrival of my father, who was sure to tell me that I now had the baby sister I had so specifically ordered--I already had two brothers, after all.

"It's a boy," he announced proudly. "He was a blue baby, not enough oxygen getting through," he added. "But we had a good doctor, he brought him around." I couldn't conceal my disappointment. "I've never seen anyone's face fall so far, so fast," he said, disappointed at my disappointment.

I remember feeling glad that this unknown little creature was OK, even though I now had an image in my head of a bright, electric blue baby boy. But I was still a little angry that he wasn't the perfect little sister I had created in my head, the one who would bring companionship and completion to my somewhat lonely life in a male-dominated world.

It would be a journey of many years before I would begin to understand what Down Syndrome even was, much less what an overwhelming effect this child would have on all our lives. In my own this included a great love I couldn't help feeling for him—how could anyone resist such a playful little creature, so cute, so black-haired and rosy-cheeked, so short and chunky, so jolly and fun? I had always loved dolls, and here was my own real live doll to play with and help care for. But later there was also an embarrassment, such as only a pre-teen or teenager can know.

My parents chose not to explain that John was different, would always be different. They thought, I think, that my brothers and I should just enjoy him as he was for as long as possible.

By the time I had figured out that he wasn't developing in the same way as his cousins of the same age, (they started walking; he didn't; they started talking; he didn't) I had entered those awful early teen years when anything that sets you apart, makes you different, even by association, was to be feared--although I never feared John, just the social ostracism that never even happened.

He wasn't supposed to live past 30 but he fooled everyone, something he loved to do throughout the 54 years of his life. He wasn't supposed to join our family either. "Put him directly into an institution," they said. "Don't even get to know him." My parents ignored that advice. He was their son and he would be going home with them, thank you very much, which is where he stayed until both had died, more than 50 years later.

Knowing my father and his "outspoken" ways (that's how people put it when they were trying to be kind), I have often wondered about the scene at the hospital when he heard those words. What would he have said? I can well imagine something like "I'll be throwing my son in the dumpster without even looking at him on the same day that you throw yours in." He wasn't one to mince words.

I didn't always appreciate Dad's colorful, attention-getting ways. Now I look back and find some of them, at least, to be heroic. He wasn't a man to spoil his kids, in fact he was a pretty tough task-master, but he did protect us--and all others who came within his purview. He was a member of the school board for 18 years, an election judge for 50 years, town clerk for I forget how many years. He was not a highly educated man himself, although self-educated through his voracious reading. My middle brother came home once, when in the third grade, with a story of having been called out of class by Mr. Maynard, the seventh grade teacher and also the principal, and brought before the entire 7th grade class to answer for the crime of shooting off caps with his finger-nails on the bus with another boy. Mr. Maynard, in front of the entire class, asked the terrified child what he thought his punishment should be, then suddenly threw him across his knee for a beating. My brother screamed and fought "like a tiger," in his words, and managed to grab a handful of black greasy hair, which his hand slid right through. "I still feel that wad of greasy hair," he recalls. My older brother, in the 7th grade class, had been attacked by Mr. Maynard with a ruler, which he succeeded in grabbing and attempting to break over his foot.

Dad was all in favor of a teacher's right to discipline and maintain or-der, but this brutality made him furious. The next day he took a break from work, still wearing his work clothes, and knocked on Maynard's classroom door. A somewhat flustered Mr. Maynard opened the door and said, "Well hello Frank--I'm teaching right now, could you come back later?"

"No," Dad said, "we need to talk right now. You can either step out here and I'll say what I have to say, or I'll come in and say it in front of your class." Mr. Maynard elected to step into the hall.

"Just want you to know," Dad said, "that if you ever physically touch a child in this school again, not just one of mine but any child, it will be your last day of work here. We have plenty of subs who can finish out the year for us. Are we clear on that?" Mr. Maynard hemmed and hawed for a moment, then muttered that he was. He finished the school year, then resigned and was never seen or heard from again. True grit, that's what Dad had.

I had had my own run-in with Mr. Maynard, who was on duty to herd us all to the right place to catch our bus home, when I was in the second grade. I made some comment, I don't remember what, that he overheard and interpreted as smart-alecky, and demanded to know who had said it.

Terrified, I remained silent. Mr. Maynard became angrier and angrier, and finally decided that a nice boy two or three years older than me, had said it, and singled him out for punishment. He denied guilt but did not tell on me. Mr. Maynard screamed that he would face terrible punishment the next day--and we all knew he meant it. We all got onto the bus, me with tears pouring down my face.

I stared hard out the window the whole way home while everyone else stared hard at me. The boy looked at me, perhaps to ask why I hadn't defended him, then felt too sorry for me to say anything, and looked away. So young to be so gallant. Many years later I heard he was dead of cancer at age 35. His younger brother, in my younger brother's class, was killed in Viet Nam.

But back to Dad, and John.

Dad wasn't one to indulge in self-pity, not for long anyway, or to rail against the universe for his bad luck. Just the previous fall, ten months before John was born, his right hand had been brutally torn off in one of those bloody farm accidents that you hear about. He was so healthy he had never even had a prescription filled, a self-professed hater of time "wasted" in a doctor's office. A hospital? Don't even think about it. Yet a hospital was, of course where he landed after the accident; after five days, when there was no more they could do for him, he didn't want to go home. He was afraid his children would find him repulsive. Upon his arrival at home, he cried, something none of us had ever seen before.

The accident happened during the fall harvest. Neighbors brought his harvest in for him. For the rest of the winter, a relatively slack time in a farmer's life, he did all that was required of him, taking care of his livestock and other chores. But this most active and physical of men, whose self-concept was based heavily on both his physical attractiveness and his competence at his job and his ability to outwork just about anyone of any age, seeming to go about his work and life as usual—spent a lot of time sitting in a chair, talking to no one, staring straight ahead. When he spoke he referred to himself as "half a man." How could he not be depressed? He had three kids old enough to be thinking about college, a fourth on the way, he soon learned, serious doubts about his current ability to make a living, and the daily frustrations of a right-handed man trying to learn to do everything over again with just one hand, and that one his left. The following spring his neighbors offered to do his spring planting for him if he wasn't up to it, but he wouldn't hear of it. He would do his share of the work and more.

With the help of a prosthesis he learned to do everything for himself except cut his meat, tie a tie, and button his right shirt cuff. Those were my jobs.

The following August, John was born.

Dad had tremendous pride in our family name, and in the piece of land that had been in the family for generations. It would be expected that he might find a child like John to be a blot on all those generations of pride and hubris. But that was not the case. They had a special bond, strengthened no doubt by their mutual love of the doomed Cubs, but also based on a kind of poorly understood mutual need. Dad, at age 39, had just suffered a disability of his own. Perhaps that gave him a sympathy, and empathy, for John that he might not otherwise have had.

Dad's last words, in the middle of the night that he died, were "John, John, John." I'm still writing poetry about them, still dealing with their lives, my complicated love for them, the loss of them.

The family passion for baseball, an almost obsessive love for a team that just couldn't win the pennant no matter what, never quite took with me, but John and Dad began every season with the elation that the Cubs would inspire with their strong beginning, then slowly petered out through the season as their annual shot at the pennant grew dimmer and dimmer until it would end with the inevitable thud every fall.

But as it was for farmers who leap from their winter hibernation and jump joyfully into a new, fresh, hopeful season every spring, so it was with the Cubs. John was a blue baby, and blue and red were his favorite colors--blue for the Cubs uniform, red for the logo. One of my brothers and his wife took John in after our parents' death, almost simultaneously with the building of their new house. Most of his wardrobe consisted, at his insistence, of Cubs hats, Cubs tee shirts, Cubs sweatshirts, Cubs jackets--well, you get the picture. His room, painted red at his insistence, became a museum to the Cubs. He especially loved Sammy Sosa. Although his speech was never very good, he could always make anyone who asked understand exactly what was happening in the current Cubs game, and exactly where the team stood at that point in the season.

John loved weddings, where it was always his hope that he would dance with the bride, and perhaps have the opportunity to do his Jackie Gleason imitation, warming up the crowd as he shook his ample belly while doing his shimmy. His final illness had begun while we were planning my daughter's wedding, for which he was trying to stay alive just for the opportunity of attending and wearing the new blue suit his oldest brother had bought him for the occasion.

He was too sick to come, and cried on the phone as we talked about it. Although he was later cremated, there was first a viewing for his life-long buddies at Opportunity House, where he had gone to school since first grade and worked in the sheltered workshop since he had been old enough to work. He was wearing the new blue suit of which he was so proud .

When my daughter was pregnant with her first child and contemplating amniocentesis, she and her husband asked what I would advise should the news turn out to be "bad." I wrestled with that question for a long time. I understood their fear, I had felt it myself. I also tried to imagine my life if John had never been in it. Would it have been better? Worse? I remember immediately breaking up with a guy who suddenly announced, out of nowhere, that he had broken up with his previous girlfriend when he learned she had a "retarded" brother. Seemed like a tragedy at the time; now I realize how lucky I was to have John there to help separate the wheat from the chaff.

Statistics tell us that today, of those women who undergo amniocentesis and discover that their fetus has Down Syndrome, 67 percent choose to abort. So there are proportionately fewer Johns in the world today, and I wonder if their parents have the same parental support groups that my parents had, or if it is so easy to fund the Opportunity Houses that make their lives happier and more productive. Recent articles tell me that a "cure," or at least the ability to modify the effects of

Down Syndrome in utero, is on the way, perhaps possible in just a few years. And the miracles of transplantation have now made it possible to restore lost limbs.

I still have no answers, and no judgements on others, whatever their decisions. I just know I loved John, and miss him still.

"I'll support whatever decision you make," I said.

So many memories:

John as a two-year-old, arms outstretched, running down the hill behind our house into my waiting outstretched arms, laughing all the way; much later, John, so sad and quiet when my parents, with him along, took me to the train station for my long overnight ride to Wilmington, Delaware, where I was to begin my first real, full-time job after college graduation; he seemed to understand that I was leaving home definitively. My parents told me later that he cried all the way home. His unabashed joy every time I came home for a visit; his unembarrassed tears and sadness every time I left again.

How much he loved his job cleaning tables at the local McDonald's. If we took him out to eat, it had to be at "his" McDonald's; his grief when they finally fired him--he had a habit of getting lost in reverie when long lines of people were waiting for a table. From then on we could only go to Steak'n Shake.

His broken heart when his girlfriend of many years, a fellow worker at Opportunity House, told him she had a new boyfriend.

I have a permanent regret, where John is concerned; on one of my last visits, when we all knew he couldn't last much longer, his hospital breakfast was served, and he lit up at the sight of one of his favorite foods--bacon. The nurse wanted him to take his medication first, then have his bacon, but he had had enough of shots and meds and was resisting. I sided with the nurse and told John he should take his medicine, as instructed. He slid down in the bed, pulled the covers over his head, and refused to come out until I left, forgoing both medicine and bacon. Why didn't I just let him enjoy his bacon?

He was a long time dying--but somehow I knew, on my last visit with him in the hospital, that it would be my last. He was weak and quiet; I couldn't think of much to say. I was sitting next to his bed. Suddenly he picked up my arm, held it to his face for a long moment, then kissed it before releasing it. I put my arms around his neck, held him close, and said, "Oh John, I love you so much." He drifted off to sleep, a smile on his face.

When I was to speak at his memorial service, I had thought about what I would say and felt confident I could say it, but upon walking up to the altar of the little country church where we had all been baptized and confirmed and where I had been married, I saw the picture of John that my brothers had placed there and I lost it. I'm not sure anyone could understand what I was saying.

Later I felt that I had not begun to do him justice, he deserved more, so I wrote a poem about him, one of those things that just wouldn't stay unwritten. It began with

> "It was the picture
> That got to me.
> The one with
> the sweet, half-sad smile
> that always told me
> He knew he was different..."

What is a life about? If it is about loving and being loved by family and friends; if it is about enjoying and pursuing a life-long passion; if it is about having fun and making people laugh; if it is about never hurting anyone, just bringing joy when you can; if it is about falling in love and getting your heart broken and going on to love again--well, he did all that.

When someone you love has been dying for a long time, you think it is still a long way off, so you don't have to think about it yet. And then when they do actually die, it comes as a terrible shock. And people think that because it has been so long in coming, you are fully prepared for it, maybe even relieved. I may have thought that myself at times. But that is not how it is.

He was a different kind of brother, but a wonderful brother neverthe-less. I hope I will be as brave and as simple when my time comes, and I hope he will be waiting with open arms, ready to fly into mine.

Meanwhile, thinking about him will always bring on the blues.

With my Blue Boy

Chapter 3

OOF DA

THEY WERE THE purest of pure Norwegians, those five daughters of Irv and Eva Gunderson, even in the small Midwestern town where their ancestors had settled, along with many other Norwegian-American immigrants—or so they thought. They didn't brag about it—Norwegians don't brag-- but they carried a quiet pride within.

Irv had never had much money but Eva, his wife, my grandmother, had been raised in a big house with hired help, one of just two spoiled girls and a spoiled brother. That didn't make his sense of failure any easier to bear (he had lost his farm, plunging the family into poverty) and yet, he was often heard to say, even in the depths of The Great Depression, in his second generation Norwegian accent, "I have five dotters, each one worth more than a million dollars." That was back when a million dollars was real money.

My Aunt Ruth was the third of the five "dotters." The oldest was Hazel, my mother, who could take yesterday's newspaper, a picture from Vogue magazine, and whatever scraps of fabric she could get her hands on and make an outfit that looked like it was imported from Paris, and fit like a glove. She kept them all looking much better than such poor people had any right to look. The others said throughout their lives that she was the one who raised them; without her good cooking, they might have starved. Without her sewing skills, they would have worn rags. In later years, she began to paint, and the houses of all her descendants are sprinkled with her exquisite watercolors.

Frances, kind, gentle Frances came next; she became a nurse and was a young single woman who visited often, before her marriage, and sang us to sleep when she did, the same songs I still sing to my grand-daughters. Fourth was Edna, whose dark-haired beauty stood out even amongst such a group of very pretty girls. They weren't called "The Five Gorgeous Gunderson Girls" for nothing. Edna loved clothes and beautiful things, of which she acquired many. When I watch a show that involves beautiful women walking the red carpet in gorgeous clothes, I often think she would be right at home—and could hold her own.

Third was Ruth, the teacher, the intellectual, the family historian and genealogist, the one who nearly wrecked her health in her single-minded determination to get an education in the midst of the depression when other young girls were happy to get a job waitressing, if they could. And last came Helen Julia, the fun-loving baby of the family, whose delicate prettiness led to a long career as a model, even as she produced six beautiful children of her own. As the only girl in a family of boys, how I loved to hang around the sisters as they drew "hosiery lines" on the backs of their long slim legs (all silk was used in the war effort), dabbed on "Evening in Paris" perfume, and even let me try on their prom dresses. Yes, I was richly blessed with aunts. I remember attending the first Gunderson family reunion to be held in 50 years, and including the entire extended clan, most of whom I didn't know. The master of ceremonies was an older man who spoke about having attended the first one, 50 years earlier. He shared many memories, then said, "And who could forget the moment when the Five Gorgeous Gunderson Girls walked in?"

But this story is about Aunt Ruth. I knew her perhaps best of all because, during my 16th summer, she offered me a job. She was widowed at a very young age and left with three young children (about 8, 5 and 3), whom she was supporting on her meager teacher's salary. But the law had suddenly changed—you now needed four years of college education, not her hard-won two, if you wanted to continue to teach. So I was to come live with her and take care of the children while she went to school. The children were adorable and I had fun with them all day, but best of all were the nights, when the children were in bed and Aunt Ruth and I talked for hours. Thank God there was no TV or I might not have had my own dreams stoked by such a person at such an impressionable age.

The only other thing, besides these beautiful daughters, that Irv and Eva had was their pride in their pure Norwegian heritage. It was believed there was just nothing better than to be Norwegian American, a combination thought to bestow the best virtues of two wonderful worlds. Norwegians were peace-loving, they didn't start wars, they were egalitarian, they adhered to the one true faith, Lutheranism . But Norwegians in America were the best of all because there was greater freedom, greater opportunity, and freedom from the class-consciousness that still stifled much of Europe.

Nevertheless, Eva often couldn't bear the burden of poverty and so many needy daughters, and was known to treat herself to the occasional nervous breakdown, requiring a minimum of six weeks of bed rest at her parents' home. When she wasn't taking the rest cure she found solace in her religion. About which she talked almost constantly. Nearly every sentence she uttered contained a reference to God and a quote from the Bible. Grandpa Irv would stand, sometimes, staring out the window with his hands in his pockets, occasionally heard to mutter "Rave on, Woman, Rave on."

And there was Uncle Burt, who had retired to his rocker in the dining room in his twenties and rarely left it. He smiled quietly, in total agreement with anything anyone said, but never worked a day in his life, nor expressed an opinion of his own.

Emotional cripples are made, not born. Uncle Burt and Grandma Eva were both tall, good-looking, well-educated for their time. Eva played the piano quite well. You could have a good conversation with the always pleasant Burt, if a bit bland as he avoided even the hint of controversy or disagreement. We always felt they both loved all of us in the family, in a vague and ineffective kind of way. But clearly, neither could cope with life. Why?

The answer lay in an ancient tragedy that had struck their father before they were born, the sainted Grandfather Bardenus, who went down in the history of Hazel's family by hitting a baseball over the barn (a feat unmatched before or since) at the age of 93.

Bardenus had fallen madly in love in his youth with a lovely young woman, also of Norwegian descent, whom he married, and lived blissfully with in a beautiful home through the births and early childhood of two children.

And then the unthinkable happened. A deadly flu epidemic pierced the aura of happiness that had heretofore protected his home, striking and killing his young wife and two children.

Devastated, he retreated into himself until he was well enough to act again, and then did what apparently was expected of a young widower in his circumstances—he numbly married his dead wife's younger sister, who was to become my great-grandmother Hannah, whom I was never to meet. Those who did remember her loved her, and spoke of the gracious and well-run home she kept, her delicious cooking, her tenderness towards children. She knew how to cope very well.

But despite outward appearances, Bardenus, a tall handsome man with a carefully trimmed mustache, respected in his community for his active and generous support of education and other civic causes, never recovered from the terrible events that had stolen his first family. He kept his second family, Eva, Burt and Helen, inside where he could keep a close eye on them. They were not to work or play, inside or out, or see other children for fear they would catch something or hurt themselves and he would again be left, devastated and alone. I remember Grandma Eva still telling us, her grandchildren, if we were playing too hard, or playing at all, that we must "come inside and rest."

Poor Uncle Burt—he did make one attempt to escape the loving but stifling atmosphere at home. He too fell in love with a lovely young woman, and came to grief because of it. I don't know her name, or how he met her, but they married and came back to Hannah and Bardenus' spacious home. Their daughter Pearl was born, apparently about nine months to the day, or perhaps less, after the wedding. Later there was talk that perhaps Burt was not the father. Shortly after the birth the young wife filed for divorce (in this straight-laced, religious town where divorce was unheard of), and left, taking their little Pearl with her. To this day, I can almost feel the pain, humiliation and grief he must have felt. It was about then that Uncle Burt retired to his rocking chair, which he rarely left, except to sleep and eat, ever again.

The sisters could see why their mother preferred life in her parents' home—so did they. It was always wonderful to visit Grandfather Bardenus and Grandmother Hannah. The house would be warm in the winter from the coal stove and big fireplace, while their little rental home would be bone-freezing cold. Grandpa and Grandma's house would be well-lit by many beautiful kerosene lamps; their own home seemed to be always dark. The smells of Grandma Hannah's roasts and baking cookies made them hungry for the real dinner that would be served. Well, they were always hungry. Ruth once told me of a Christmas dinner, yes, Christmas dinner, that consisted of plain noodles, nothing more. I don't think they were even buttered.

So it should come as no surprise that Ruth spent as much time at her grandparents' spacious home as she could. In addition to the smell of polish on gleaming woodwork, as opposed to the smell of garbage at home, there were nooks and crannies everywhere, each one a repository of some piece of family history. Her family had moved from one ever-cheaper rental to another too often to accumulate much of anything.

Best of all was the attic, full of trunk after trunk of yellowed hand-made linens, Grandmother's hand-embroidered wedding dress and trousseau, musty but still beautiful leather-bound books, dried flowers from wedding bouquets, Grandmother Hannah's gorgeous wedding veil, hats fit for the Queen of England that had once sat upon Grandmother's glossy black hair, which had never been cut and which she wore twisted into low buns. It still had very little grey when she died at nearly 90 years of age.

For Ruth's 15th summer, Grandmother Hannah, knowing of her love of family history and her curiosity about their origens, invited her to come stay with her awhile and help clean out that attic. Even she was curious about what might be in some of those trunks, which hadn't been opened in decades. Some she had inherited and stored without ever getting around to opening.

Ruth was entranced by the spinning wheel that had come over on the ship with her family in the early 1830's and which was later a fixture in her sister Hazel's home, then in my older brother's, and the beautiful mantel clock that her great-grandfather had bought with his first American paycheck, now residing in my younger brother's home.

And then they opened the trunk full of letters, written in archaic Norwegian. While they were instilled with pride in their "pure" Norwegian heritage, they really had little or no Norwegian custom, culture or language after several generations as Americans. Eva would say "oof da" (an untranslatable exclamation that every Norwegian or person of Norwegian descent will recognize—when the rest of the language has been lost, oof da remains, making us the butt of many jokes) as she tossed out the "grupse" (garbage) after every meal, and they faithfully attended the local Lutheran church, full of other Norwegian Americans much like themselves—but that was about it. The letters might as well have been written in some obscure code. Some appeared to be tear-stained. Ruth immediately wanted to hear those voices from the past.

Too soon, her wonderful summer ended and she had to go home and back to school. But she couldn't get the letters off her mind. Who had written them? What did they say?

One of her teachers in her little mostly Norwegian-American school had graduated from St. Olaf's College, a liberal arts school in Minnesota, which just happened to be owned and run by the Lutheran Church of America and located right in the heart of the Norwegian-American diaspora. Perhaps he would know someone who could read and translate the letters? It just happened that he did.

After months of agonizing waiting to receive and read his translations— they were life-changing. My great-great-great grandmother had written them to the beloved younger son who was departing for America, most likely never to be seen by her again. Nor, she knew, would she ever meet her future daughter-in-law or grandchildren. Fascinated, Ruth began learning everything she could about Norwegian history and our family's roots there, knowing that one day, when she could, she would travel there and seek out relatives, however distant.

She frowned as she learned of the racial prejudice against the "northern people," then called Laplanders, that had scarred Norway's history as surely as it had scarred so many others.

Ruth immediately began learning what she could of the Laps, who now consider that a derogatory name, as they were so discriminated against and so disenfranchised for so many centuries. They are called Sami now, their name since prehistoric stone age times, when they settled the land that comprises the northernmost parts of Norway, Sweden, Finland and Russia. These indigenous pre-historic peoples were reindeer-herders for centuries (although only about 10 percent still practice), as well as fishermen and sheepherders. They were an embarrassment to Norway and the other European countries they inhabited, and as such were stripped of rights and (resource-rich) land, saw their children kidnapped and raised in boarding schools, were forcefully sterilized by government doctors, and in general endured the sad litany of hardship forced upon the oppressed everywhere.

They are thought of as people of the far north, but as early as the 13th century, when the Black Plague killed about 60 percent of the Norwegian population, they began moving southward along the "plague lines.' Norwegians suffered much more than the Sami from the Plague, as they traded, by land and sea, with other European countries, as the Sami did not, and they were much more densely populated, fertile breeding grounds for the Plague. When the horror finally subsided, leaving a weakened and depopulated Norway in its wake, some of the Sami people began moving southward and into the deserted homes. There are Sami people living in those same stone houses from the 13th century to this day. And who knows how many Norwegians have Sami blood? It is not talked about. It appears that to be human means you are not "pure" anything—and that is really OK.

But great-great-great grandmother spoke of other things in her letters.

"My Dearest Son," she wrote. "I stood on the dock waving at your departing ship until it sank over the horizon and I could see it no more. And then I stood there for another couple of hours, until the sun went down, praying for your safety and well-being, asking God to give me the strength to live without you. Already life here seems even more lonely and barren than it was before. "

There was more, of course, and many similar letters through the years, but they always ended with the same words. "We pray that one day you will come back. We await your return. Love, Mother."

Life went on, though the words in the letters stayed in Ruth's mind. She worked her way through the nearby state teachers' college, with the help of a scholarship, worked for 40 years as an elementary school teacher, married, had three children. She was widowed twice, and thus entered her retirement years alone. It was then she decided to fulfill her long-held dream of travel, and of course Norway was to be her first stop. She did her research (she had after all been the family historian and genealogist for years) and located the village from which our family had sprung, and some distant relatives living there still.

It felt like coming home. People looked like her. She had brought the letters of the woman who was their ancestress as well as ours, and was able to tell them, "You see, one of us did come back."

She talked about what she had learned about the Sami, and found that attitudes as well as lifestyles had changed in this beautiful, once poor but now rich country. There was no longer any embarrassment about possible Sami forbears, only embarrassment about their own prejudice, and about the way the Sami had been treated for so many centuries.

And back home was the same. A new generation was not "pure" anything, just the usual American polyglot, and that was just fine. One of the fun things she learned was that some well-known people, including Renee Zellweger and Joni Mitchell, are of mixed Norwegian and Sami heritage.

Aunt Ruth died too young, at age 64, of ovarian cancer, but the legacy she left lives on. We all know more about ourselves and our history and how we became who we are because of her work. Every family (and perhaps every politician) needs a Ruth to remind them of their heritage and its many sources, and to think of the complicated personal and family story that accompanies every immigrant.

That would be all of us.

Postscript; Like so many others, I recently sent some spit in to ancestry.com. Turns out I am 50 percent Norwegian—no surprise there. But I am also, according to this report, one percent "Finland/North Russia..." ancient home of the Sami people.

Chapter 4

ɷɷ

PARADISE LOST

"**WILL YOU MARRY** me?" he asked. "Of course," he added, "it would involve moving to Venezuela three months from now....." Was it a function of youth, ignorance, or true love that I said "yes" almost immediately?

I don't know, but I've never looked back and now, nearly a half century later, I can say I have no regrets. I didn't think about the fact that I did not speak Spanish, had never been out of the United States, knew absolutely nothing about Venezuela, would have to give up my car, job, live far from family and friends. I just thought it sounded like an exciting adventure, and kind of assumed we would be back and resume "real life" after a couple of years. It was an exciting adventure...that stretched into nearly 12 years and three countries. But it had been his constant world travels, his fluency in several languages, his knowledge of a world I had only read about, that had first attracted me to Jim.

We met at a Chicago Tribune (where I was working as a reporter) after-work party at my apartment; a colleague had called and said a fraternity brother was in town—could he bring him along? I said sure. At first I wasn't too interested because I thought he was too young for me—he is in fact two years younger, but he looked younger still. But the third time he called he said, "This is your last chance—I'm leaving for Viet Nam in a week and won't be back for three months." Well, what did I have to lose? If I didn't like him, I would never see him again anyway.....but of course, I did like him, and he liked me, and we went out every night that week, and then he left (a pattern which continues to this day, I might add).

I thought, "Oh great, I finally meet someone I like, but we barely know each other and this fledgling relationship will never survive a three-month separation." This was before email, cheap international phone calls, cell phones. But he surprised me. Nearly every day during those three months I got a telegram, or a letter on that pale blue air mail stationary (remember?) or had flowers awaiting me at my apartment—or something. Who could resist that? I started racing home after work to see what he had done this time. I couldn't do the same in return for him because this was a business trip, he was in a different city and hotel every day or two. When he finally returned, bearing a beautiful gold and jade bracelet and a book of Shakespeare's sonnets, I admit I was impressed.

This went on for two and a half years before we got to the "Will you marry me" part. After a beautiful but rather quickly thrown together wedding (we only had three months to plan it, and the move; my parents, and Jim's, who hosted a wonderful night-before dinner) did a heroic job of coming up with a nice wedding on the spur of the moment, two days after Christmas, no less. We stopped in the Caribbean for a honeymoon, then flew on to Maiquetia International Airport, located on the Venezuelan coast. It would be a long drive straight uphill to Caracas, the capital city, where we would be living. Its location, nearly straddling the equator but high in the mountains, gave it an ideal climate that never really changed, except in the most minor ways. Most equatorial locations are unbearably hot, but Caracas' location in the mountains kept the temperature hovering around 70 degrees, all the time. Most days there would be a light rainfall for about 20 minutes, and when it ended everything would be sparkling and smelling of the ever-blooming flowers. The climate was so perfect that our first apartment had several windows with no glass—with no flying insects (we'll get to the cockroaches later), no wind, rainfall that fell straight down, there was just no need for glass. For two people accustomed to the brutal winters of the northern Midwest, this in itself was quite amazing. And so were the year-around long beautiful sunny days that would end with a final cafecito on the Sabana Grande late at night,

But first we had to get from the airport to the hotel where we would be living for the next three months. On that long slow crawl up the mountain to the city, we passed mile after mile of "ranchitos," or little huts made of scrap corrugated metal, scrap wood, and anything else their residents could find. I had never seen poverty quite like this, and it was shocking. I was to learn that every time there was a heavy rainfall, which did happen from time to time, these poorly built little houses would come sliding down the mountainside, wreaking destruction as they went. My enthusiasm for my new home was beginning to dampen.

But then we arrived at The Tamanaco Hotel, probably Latin America's premium hotel at that time. Everything was beautiful—our room, the food, the vistas of mountain and city, the huge sparkling pool where, it seemed, much of the city gathered for drinks, lunch, conversation. The ever-present flower gardens everywhere, throughout the year and, it seemed, throughout the city, kept a heavenly haze of fragrance infusing all of daily life. We were there for three months, awaiting our shipment of possessions and a suitable apartment. Jim had been doing business in Venezuela for several years, spoke fluent Spanish, and had good friends who immediately became my friends too.

Becoming acquainted with Venezuela's coffee culture was an unexpected bonus. Like its next door neighbor Colombia, Venezuela grew some of the best coffee in the world. Unlike Colombia, which depended heavily on coffee exports for its income, Venezuela had oil and gold to sell, and kept its best coffee for its own use. Not only was it incredibly delicious, but there were about 20 different ways to order it; you couldn't just say "coffee, please." It could be marron, marroncito, con leche, espresso—and so many others I can't remember. What you ordered depended upon your personal taste and the time of day. At the time, we in the States were drinking what the Venezuelans called "brown water." This was before Starbucks brought great coffee experiences to everyone.

I began studies at the Centro Cultural Venezolano Americano on the Monday after our Friday arrival in January of 1970. Classes, which included lessons in Venezuelan history and culture as well as the Spanish language, were enlightening and fun, providing me with intellectual stimulation as well as the chance to meet and become friends with people from all over the world, Dutch, German, Italian, Israeli, some of them friends to this day. I found that I loved learning a language and was pretty good at it, although never as good as Jim. But there was one great frustration: no matter how well I did on homework assignments, verb conjugations, tests, and I did do well, I would go out on the street to use my new-found abilities—and no one understood a word I said. Nor did I understand them. And lovely as hotel life was, I was a new bride and dying to set up housekeeping and see and use my own things again, especially the wedding presents I had barely had a chance to glance at before we left.

And it finally happened—we found a three bedroom two bath apartment in a building built into a mountainside, with spectacular views of both mountains and city from our little balcony. It was in a high rise building in a section of the city called Colinas de Bello Monte—hills of the beautiful mountain, which is exactly what it was, a foothill of a beautiful mountain. The building itself was less romantically named—Residencias Tecnicas. And it had its own beautiful pool, used daily by pretty much everyone in the building, giving me a wonderful chance to meet and get to know my Venezuelan neighbors—we were the only non-Venezuelans in the building.

I was walking to the parking lot one day when a young and beautiful woman I had often seen around said "Hello, how are you?" using her few words of English. She was exotic in a way I had never seen before, long, shiny black hair swinging almost to her waist, thick bangs that nearly obscured her eyes, a swing to her walk that denoted energy, joy, a freely shared love of life. Her name was Angela, I learned, and we were instant best friends, as we remain to this day. My loneliness ended at that moment. From then on we zoomed through Caracas in her little red convertible, top down, on a nearly daily basis, sometimes to pick up her kids at school, sometimes to do errands, sometimes taking off for a day at the beach.

I still see them because, like everyone with any resources, they left Venezuela when it was clear the Socialist/Communist takeover was going to bring the starvation and repression we see today in this once thriving and stable country.

Yes, there was the aforementioned poverty back then, as there is everywhere, including here in the US. But there was also hope, education and health care, a growing and thriving middle class, a stable democratic government (the oldest democracy in Latin America), a friendly relationship with western industrialized countries, based on shared Judeo-Christian values, a stable currency—and certainly no starvation. It is reported that last year (2017) the average Venezuelan lost 37 pounds. The thousands incarcerated in filthy prisons for having dissented are no doubt a lot thinner than that. The national currency, the Bolivar, was four Bs (as they were called) to the dollar, and stayed that way the entire three years we were there. According to Mary Anastasia O'Grady's column in the Jan. 22, 2018 Wall Street Journal, the minimum monthly wage is now 797,510 Bolivars, which the day before was worth $3.90. This in a country that sits on the greatest deposits of oil in the world, and has other huge resources of gold and coffee. I had major abdominal surgery in Caracas, in a fine hospital, with no ensuing problems. Today people are dying of treatable diseases for lack of even the most basic medical supplies. The terrible destruction of a beautiful country is a book that someone else will have to write.

I can only tell you what it once was, and thus how far it has fallen. But I recommend O'Grady's column if you want to get a fuller picture. The great Simon Bolivar, Founder and Liberator, would be in tears if he could hear Hugo Chavez and his henchman refer to what has happened to Venezuela as a "Bolivarian Revolution."

Back to Residencias Tecnicas—I continued to attend daily classes at The Centro Cultural (each class lasted six weeks, and there were six levels), I completed all six. After we moved into our apartment and began to meet and become friends with Venezuelans, a miracle happened. After school, I would come home and begin speaking Spanish with Venezuelans, as they for the most part did not speak English, and within a very short time—I understood them and they understood me! Total immersion, combined with the grammar learned in school, is really the only way to learn a language. For me it was, and still is, an indescribable thrill to find myself conversing easily in a foreign language. I still spend some of my time teaching English to newcomers to this country, using the empathy and skills learned during my years overseas.

One of the best things about living in a country other than my native country was the exposure to multiculturalism long before that word was in vogue. Every event, every dinner party involved people from all over the world; multiple languages were being spoken. And conversation was usually about world events. This was true for our eight years in Latin America and our three years in Europe and creates an atmosphere we continue to seek out to this day.

As childless newlyweds, our years in Venezuela were all about fun, in a country of remote and perfect beaches, jungles full of exotic animals, including 427 different types of mammals, giant anteaters, jaguars, howler monkeys , stunning scenery, 30 minute flights to such weekend getaways as Aruba (then an undeveloped island of spectacular beaches and a couple of little Mom and Pop restaurants and motels), Isla Margarita, and other small, beautiful undeveloped islands. The Avila Mountain loomed over Caracas, giving it much of its mystique and charm. A cable car would take you to the top, where you could enjoy the views for a while and then either take it back down again or hike back down—or you could catch the one that would take you down the other side where a pristine beach awaited you., returning the same way, in reverse. Not a bad way to spend a day, as we did so many times.

We adored Angela and her husband Oscar's two beautiful little daughters. I felt honored to be included in their annual Christmas tradition when, as in all Venezuelan homes, all the women of the family, of every generation, gathered to make hallacas and other traditional Christmas foods. The hallacas in particular were labor intensive as well as delicious, and I had a wonderful time with Angela, her mother, her mother-in-law, her husband's two aunts and her two daughters as we chopped, kneaded, rolled, wrapped and fried the many minced vegetable and meat ingreadients. When completed they were wrapped in dough, then wrapped again in banana leaves and steamed before serving. They serve them to me still when I visit them in Miami, where they now live. I also loved the wonderful street food available everywhere—every type of arepa, empanada, jugo de cana, pan de jamon. I was beginning to feel like a real Venezuelan.

And there was the jungle and the beautiful, isolated beaches; part of the Amazon jungle is in Venezuela, dotted with hard to get to waterfalls and hundreds of different types of exotic animals, some found nowhere else.

Venezuelans were, in general, charming, fun, outgoing, always ready for a good time—and focused on appearance. I quickly learned that going anywhere, even for a quick run to the grocery for a few eggs, meant looking your absolute best, whether that called for a casual or dressy look. I don't believe I ever saw a Venezuela woman having a "bad hair day,' or not perfectly dressed and accessorized, whether that meant a gorgeous dress for late nights on the Sabana Grande or skin-tight jeans with just the right boots and jacket. Not looking your best at all times, regardless of your socio-economic status, was a cultural no-no. I continue to follow that dictum, with varying degrees of success, to this day, and have found that it does make life better, even on bad days.

All this was, fortunately, accompanied by a great sense of humor. Anyone who has ever lived in, or moved to, an interesting place will tell you that a by-product of that move is entertaining many houseguests, usually a great pleasure as you take the time to do and see things that you might not do otherwise. With one of those guests, we planned a day at one of the beautiful beaches, then a stop for dinner at a seafood place on the coast that we had heard was wonderful, not only for the food but for the magnificent views of the ocean as it was perched on a high cliff.

We walked in and immediately spotted a set table, empty, next to the wall that separated the restaurant from the huge waves, perhaps 50 feet high, that regularly came crashing up to, but not over, the wall. We immediately wanted that table, the closest to the wall, and thus the ocean view; the headwaiter shook his head discouragingly; no, he indicated, we really didn't. "But we do!" we insisted. "Is it reserved?" "No," he replied, but he would rather seat us elsewhere. We insisted and he gave in. We were seated, ordered our fabulous seafood lunch, complete with an excellent Portuguese wine, and were just finishing (fortunately) when a truly gigantic wave came crashing up and over the wall (apparently it did do that occasionally, but only in the exact spot where our table was situated—so why was there a table there anyway?). We were suddenly sitting there, soaking wet, tartar sauce in our hair, etc. We sat in stunned silence for a moment, then burst into hysterical laughter. We had apparently passed some kind of test, because everyone in the restaurant applauded loudly and from then on drinks (ours, at least) were on the house.

But all good things must end, to make way for the next exciting chapter, and after three years we learned that we were being transferred to Brazil, where Jim had been offered a challenging new job. We had sold all extraneous things and sent the rest on to Brazil, moved out of our apartment and back to the Tamanaco Hotel, from where we were to catch a cab next morning to Maiquetia Airport where our flight to Sao Paulo, Brazil, would await us.

But life is always full of surprises, isn't it. We got a phone call that night, that very night, from Bensenville Home Society in Bensenville, Ill., telling us they had a baby girl for us ("unusually pretty, in my opinion," the social worker said.) Did we want her? You bet we did.. And thus began a love affair that lasts to this day.

ROSEBUD

"She's an unusually pretty baby…"
a voice crackled across the continents
"Do you want her?" "Did we want her????"
We asked, incredulously.

Plans changed
An airplane in the opposite direction.
A blur of relatives and then
Alone, we go to meet her.

Nature contributes to our joyous party
With a burnished gold sun,
A cobalt April sky.
It's Spring—always my favorite season.

She's an angel with a rosebud mouth
Eyes that outblue the sky,
Smelling of milk and baby powder
And new clothes

Skin feeling as soft
As her new flannel jammies.
It's love at first sight
And this one will last.

"Hello Elizabeth! Thank you for choosing us."

On to the next adventure. Brazil awaits.

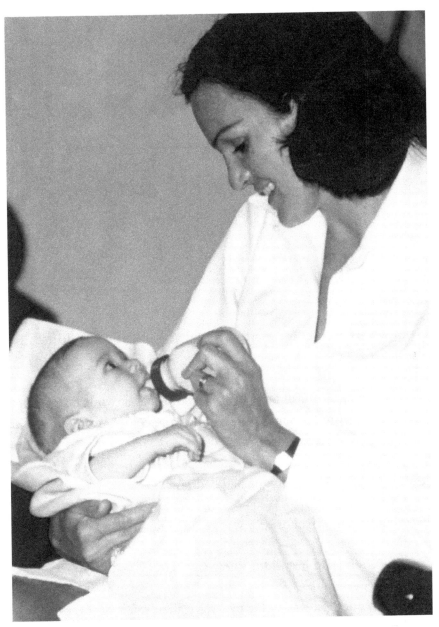

First Feeding

Chapter 5

———❧———

THE FLYING CARPET

By Linda Klein Means

HERE ARE MY excuses for ever owning that god-awful rug in the first place:

We were living in Brazil because Jim, my husband, worked in the international division of a major U.S. health care company. There weren't that many consumer choices;

It was the seventies—everyone had bad taste;

Everyone we knew had one, or was getting one;

We were young and just didn't know any better.

The rug in question was a nine by twelve affair made of sheepskin, the wool probably five or six inches thick and weighing God knows how many pounds. You'd see one in someone else's house and it would look so thick, so luxurious, so elegant, clear evidence that these adventurous souls had traveled the world, tasted the exotic, left boring subdivisions with cheap factory-made wall-to-wall carpeting behind. Didn't those words just fit us to a T?

My husband was as excited about our getting our own magical rug as I was. Unfortunately, as it turned out, his enthusiasms, once kindled, didn't die as easily.

The rug was delivered to the tiny house we were living in with our two year old daughter, soon to be joined by an infant brother. It looked great, Baby Girl loved the softness, it provided a wonderful place to spread out with the Sunday papers, everyone was happy.

But soon I noticed that it was difficult, nay impossible to clean. Have you ever tried to vacuum a five-inch-deep pile?

"Clean?" my husband would say. "But don't we have maids to clean?"

Well, let me tell you about Brazilian maids. First of all, we are Midwesterners, people who don't usually have or grow up with maids, so there's a learning curve. Yes, we did have maids to clean, everyone did, not only the live-in who might do the cooking, the laundry, light housekeeping, possibly some baby-sitting, but also a faxioneira, or cleaning lady who came weekly to do the heavy work (the maid's maid," my husband called her).

There were no good products or appliances to make housekeeping doable, and among the Brazilian families we socialized with children were not encouraged to babysit, mow lawns, or take other first small jobs so common among American teenagers; in fact, putting their young out to work would have been considered a terrible disgrace, an admission that the family's finances and honor had fallen to the bottom rung. And evenings at restaurants and other people's homes NEVER included children; thus dependence on live-in maids was part of the acculturation process; it was part of living in Brazil and, as with everything else, it took some getting used to. In this class-based society a woman either had a maid or was one—and if you had one, you likely always had, and had well-established ways of dealing with one.

We expats came in clueless, and made mistakes. We paid too much, out of feelings of guilt for what felt like exploitation, thus setting a new standard that Brazilians were unable or unwilling to meet, and setting ourselves up for reverse exploitation. We tried too hard to be buddy-buddy, for the same reasons and with similar results—everyone was uncomfortable.

And like our wealthier Brazilian acquaintances, we rarely thought of these maids as people, with lives, stories, families and troubles of their own. Whether they were good at what they did, or not so good, they made our lives possible, and were an endless source of amusing stories.

And the young girls from poor families in the countryside whom we could afford were just as much expats in our homes as we were in their country, just as clueless about how to deal with this strange new world as we were. To them, we with our company-subsidized homes and cars and travel and reputations as "rich Americans," who paid more than Brazilians, were wealthy, yet unlike the truly wealthy Brazilians, we barbecued, dressed casually, raised our own children, and cooked—sometimes, at least. And the wealthier Brazilians we socialized with found us just as strange.

And so, with a few notable exceptions, we expats stuck together, like expats everywhere, and made our mistakes together, and laughed about them together. But when I think back on those maids, I think we were more alike than we realized, both strangers in strange lands, always making silly mistakes, providing fodder for other people's jokes.

Being young, inexperienced, and still close to the bottom rung of the corporate ladder, we were not yet fully aware that you got what you paid for. And what we paid for was the bottom rung of the domestic help ladder—often illiterate, always totally inexperienced teenage girls just in from small rural towns or farms to make their fortune and find a husband in the big city.

Martina, for example, had never seen or heard of a telephone before, and would slap her forehead and scream "Aye, meu Deus no ceu!" (Oh my God in Heaven!) every time it rang. Pretty soon the aforementioned two year old daughter was slapping her forehead and saying, in her little tiny two-year-old voice, "Aye, meu Deus no ceu!" every time the phone rang. I finally succeeded in teaching Martina to pick up the phone and answer it, but it took a lot longer to get her to stop hanging up immediately after saying, "Yes, Dona Linda is right here, I'll call her."

And there was Marianna. We had a collie dog then; I was going to be out for most of the day and asked Marianna to take him for a walk. Who knew that Brazilian maids considered that the lowest task on earth, grounds for quitting, which she promptly did? Later we found crossed chicken bones at the foot of one of our trees, a sure sign that we had been the recipients of a Condomble curse. Condomble is a religion based on a mix of Catholicism, the official religion of Brazil, and an African spiritualism brought over by slaves a couple of centuries earlier. Yemanja, the goddess of the sea, and The Virgin Mary, for example, have become conflated, sharing characteristics and rituals.

Our family now included an infant son, an abandoned baby from a Brazilian Catholic orphanage, just three days old but dying, if he didn't get help soon, from an infection picked up at birth in a poorly equipped hospital, a wildly hyperactive Collie dog, a rescued cat who immediately produced a batch of kittens, and a guinea pig called Pipoca (popcorn in Portuguese) but generally referred to as our watch pig.

I tried to divest ourselves of some of the kittens. All Brazilian lojas, or small neighborhood pharmacies/general stores, had resident cats, it seemed to be an unwritten law, and of course those untended cats would have kittens. I spoke to our local lojero about accepting one of our unwanted kittens, thus unleashing a torrent of unedited outrage in Brazilian Portuguese, roughly translated as, "Are you out of your mind? Do you think I am running an animal farm? Do I look like I need more hungry cats around here? Would you be offering to come over and feed this pack of wild, always hungry ingrates? Holy Mother of God!"

This is one of the ways in which you begin to pick up the local patois.

If you went early in the morning to one of these places, you could have your morning coffee, a small but very potent espresso, standing up at the bar while listening in on the conversation of a crew of workmen starting their day with a shot of whiskey washed down with beer—and then the espresso.

But a great thing about those lojas (I thought at the time, being as I've already pointed out, young and not that smart) was that you never really needed to see a doctor. You would just go to your lojero, tell him about your sore throat, or cough, or whatever, and he would give you a shot of antibiotic and just like that whatever was ailing you was gone. And things were sold one at a time. If you wanted gum, or aspirin, or cigarettes, (yes, people still smoked back then) he would say, "How many?"

And you might walk away with a stick of gum, perhaps three or four cigarettes, and half dozen aspirin.

Anyway, we needed more space.

After much searching, we lucked into a huge (to us) gorgeous Portuguese Colonial house, complete with hand-painted kitchen tiles, stucco exterior, red-tiled roof, porches, verandas, a gigantic marble bathroom which little girls soon learned was a great place to play "seals" if they splashed a lot of water on the floor, got naked, and used their "flippers" to shoot themselves all the way across the floor on their tummies.

We couldn't wait to install the fabulous rug, along with the rest of our stuff. It all looked better in the new, larger, fire-placed living room.

My husband remained as enamored as ever with it, but I was slowly becoming disenchanted. You still couldn't really clean the damn thing, and stuff was piling up in there, no pun intended. I was beginning to hate what I now referred to as "that freakin' rug," and to secretly plot its demise at the next transfer to another country, which was bound to come up soon.

It did, and to Paris, no less. It would be hard to say which I was more excited about, moving to Paris or freeing myself of that rug. But my husband had originally noted that I wanted one, and had brought it home as a surprise--and I had loved it--but now hated to tell him that I no longer did. After pointing out to him that, sad though it was, we couldn't take the rug with us--it was filthy, wearing out, we were leaving our lovely big house for what would no doubt be apartment living in France, who knew how much space we would have, etc., he reluctantly agreed that we should get rid of it before the move. Which I promptly did. Someone bought it at our final sale.

But life is nothing if not full of surprises.

On moving day, yes, on moving day itself, he came home with a big grin on his face and said, and I quote, "I knew how unhappy you were about having to give up the rug, and I knew we would never find another one in Paris—so I bought you a new one! They're loading it on the truck right now!" Sure enough, two burly men were straining to get the huge and disgusting thing into the moving van. It had already begun the first leg of its journey to Paris. And soon we would begin ours.

THE CITY OF LIGHT

The plain, flat-out gorgeousness of Paris hit me over the head on our first night there, tired though we were from the move and the long plane flight. We toured the city at night with everything lit up, in that unique Parisian way, and there it all was, glowing like gold: the Louvre, the Eiffel tower, the Conciergerie (still my favorite), the Champs Elysees, the Seine, undulating and glittering through it all like a diamond necklace from Cartier, Notre Dame--I felt as though I had landed in the middle of a fairy tale. Was this really where I would be living for the next few years?

The history, the art, the beauty, the food and wine, the bread and croissants, have all been written about in countless books and articles by both the famous and infamous--so I will confine myself to relating just a few of the curious, or strange, or bizarre (when seen through the eyes of a newbie foreigner) or just fascinating things that can happen.

We were Americans, yes, but having just spent the previous eight years in two countries of Latin America, and having both become fluent in two Latin languages, we thought we were fully prepared for life pretty much anywhere. We weren't. Well, perhaps Jim was. He had spent a year abroad, in Colombia, South America, during his teenage years, at which time he fell in love with international living, and discovered that he had a natural gift for learning languages and assimilating into different cultures, and knew then that that would be his life. Me not so much. My life since college had been spent writing for newspapers; everyone I had dated since then until meeting Jim had been newspapermen, and I always assumed that was where my life would be. But no. Here I was with an international businessman, struggling to keep up. But I had also always had a deep desire to travel and see the world, but didn't know how I would ever do that on my salary. And here was someone who was showing me more than I ever even knew existed. I discovered that I also enjoyed learning languages and was pretty good at it.

Sometime during that first week, while we were still living in a hotel with our two small children and an au pair, I decided to take everyone to the Champs Elysees for our first real Parisian lunch. We found what appeared to be a modest little cafe with outdoor seating and a beautiful view of the Arc de Triomph. We all ordered ham sandwiches and Coke (with difficulty--my French was in the VERY early stages, the waiter was like a stereotypical French waiter from an old movie, with nothing but contempt for someone who murdered the language and didn't know the correct way of doing things--I was to learn that there is a rule for EVERYTHING in France) and it was without doubt the most delicious sandwich I had ever tasted, possibly unrivaled to this day. The long, slim crusty on the outside but soft and chewy on the inside baguette was so fresh it was still hot. The thin slices of prosciutto and ementhaler cheese were unbelievable. And French butter is in a class of its own. We all thoroughly enjoyed this spectacular treat--until the bill came. This was 1978, and the bill was well over $100, (a fortune to us at the time) and all we had had was four sandwiches and four cokes. Jimmy Carter was president and the value of the dollar (the currency in which we were paid) was at an all-time low. This is how I learned that you never eat in a spot that has a beautiful view of a famous monument, unless you have an unlimited budget. The food will be just as wonderful at a more out-of-the-way location.

Paris was so walkable, and with a Plan de Paris in hand it was easy to take the Metro everywhere. There are 315 miles of underground Metro (subway) in Paris, one of the oldest transport systems in the world. And being French, they combine beauty with utility. The Art Deco-style wrought iron arches that introduce each station are works of art in themselves, and many of the stops, in particular that to the fabulous Louvre, are practically art museums in their own right. And the little brown book known as the Plan de Paris makes it easy for even non-French-speaking foreigners to be transported in more ways than one—from one place to another, from one world to another, all in the space of from ten minutes to an hour.

When weekends came we would pile into our little Renault and explore the countryside--Bourgogne, Normandy, Lorraine, the south of France (on longer trips)—as we would tell our frequent houseguests, "Just take off in any direction; it's all good." This became even easier and more fun when we discovered an equally wonderful little book called "Weekend et Vacance a la Ferme"—sort of a rural French precursor to Airbnb. You would stay in a wonderful old rural French home, sometimes hundreds of years old, from which you could take off for day trips after a delicious French breakfast, always including the incomparable bread, homemade jam, and une Grand Crème (best coffee in the world) before returning to what would surely be a spectacular home-cooked dinner. Or you could stick around, get to know the family, practice your French, help out on the farm and with dinner preparations—we did some of both and enjoyed it all.

On one of those day trips in Normandy we noticed gigantic metal grates being used in fields to cover swampy areas and ditches to allow cattle to cross without getting mired. We asked about them over dinner and learned thy were leftover detritus from the Allied landing, used to transport troops from ships, across beaches, to land—being shot at every step of the way of course.

As with our lives in Venezuela and Brazil, it was through friends and school that we learned about the country and the language in a way that we never could have from a tour.

Mme. Henri-Martin, a resident of our 17th arrondisement apartment building (such was the formality of her generation of French women that I never did learn her first name, nor did she learn mine) approached me one day to tell me, in French, that she would really like to improve her English. Would I be interested in joining her for lunch one day a week, with us conversing in French for my benefit one week, and in English for hers the next? Yes, of course I would be, and she told me so many interesting, and sometimes horrific, stories of life during the German occupation, the all-pervasive fear, the difficulty of finding food.

But best of all was the opportunity to study at The Sorbonne, France's oldest and probably best university, whose primary campus is located right in the heart of Paris' most exciting and bohemian section, The Quartier Latin (Latin Quarter). Its two year course of study, designed specifically for foreigners but taught only in French, covered French language, history and culture. It was taught in the French top-down system, totally driven by teacher lectures, emphasis on correct verb conjugations, memorization of facts, much homework, readings from the Western Canon. But the material was fascinating, the class met for three hours every day, students were from everywhere, but with a large number from the US and from former French colonies in Africa. It was dense, challenging, a bit heavy on the pressure, and I loved it. And if you didn't know a lot more at the end than you did at the beginning, it was because you weren't trying very hard . Once again, it was good teaching combined with near total immersion that resulted in fluency in a language.

But best of all was heading off for a coffee after with classmates. You were in the Quartier Latin, steps from the Musee Cluny, an undervis-ited piece of the Medieval world, with what is probably the greatest collection of Medieval tapestries in the world, a little jewel of a Picasso Museum, the Marais, exquisite little coffee shops redolent of great cof-fee, ethnic restaurants from everywhere, street markets, and all that makes Paris Paris. Best of all was the conversation—about politics, art, cultural events, goals, dreams. But suddenly it would be near time that another kind of school, that of my children, would be letting out, and I would head back to the Metro and take it to the Argentine, the one nearest my home, in the shadow of the Arc de Triomph, to meet my children, who had spent their day at the Ecole Bilangue, located in the beautiful Parc Monceau, which they shared with Sophia Loren's son, Eduardo, and that of Loren and Hemingway biographer A.E. Hotchner. Catching a glimpse of Sophia herself, through the tinted glass of her limousine, was always a thrill.

We had, after three years in Paris, been overseas, in three countries, learning three new languages and cultures, for nearly 12 years, and I was ready to go home. Despite its romantic reputation, Paris is cold, grey and rainy for much of the year. Summer, with its long bright days, is a marvel, but it is short. Winter, with its short, dark, bone-chilling days, is long. I was getting homesick. I was not sorry to learn we were moving again—this time to California. Speaking of culture shock.....

But first we needed to get rid of a lot of stuff—furniture that was getting old, outgrown toys and clothing—and of course, the aforementioned rug.

The French, I was told, did not do yard sales, garage sales, call them what you will. "Well," I said to myself, "I'm not French and I'm having one." I put an ad in our local paper, and another on the bulletin board at our children's school, with little expectation that anyone would come. I couldn't have been more wrong—tout Paris turned out for this little slice of Americana.

Best of all was a tall (as in maybe seven feet) charming young Nigerian man with the deepest, darkest, most beautiful ebony skin I had ever seen. He fell in love at first sight with the sheepskin rug, but was afraid it would be too expensive for him. I was a motivated seller and prepared to offer an excellent price. We struck a deal. It would be difficult to say which of us was happier.

But then a problem arose—how would he get it home? Or even out of our second floor apartment, reached by one of those tiny wrought iron cage elevators found in 19th century French apartment buildings, so long on charm but so short on utility? I have no idea how many pounds that thing weighed when rolled up, and at nine feet long it would take two or more strong men to carry it out. And he didn't have a car to put it in. We called a taxi, whose driver looked at it, gave a Gallic shrug and said "Mais non," lit a Galois and drove away. Fortunately, a family equipped with a truck had been buying some things, and agreed to give my new friend and his new rug a ride if we could just get it to the street.

We looked at each other and both knew, without words, what we were going to do. We checked the street below to make sure it was clear and together managed, with me at one end and him at the other, to hoist it onto the top of the wrought iron balcony, and to throw the rug out through the tall, elegant French windows, over the railing, and down to the street below. Some people didn't like that very much but heck, I was leaving anyway.

Chapter 6

THE LADY ON THE SEINE

NOWHERE IS THE ancient and complicated relationship between France and the United States better illustrated than in the history of The American Church in Paris, an English-language American Protestant church located in the heart of Catholic, French speaking France.

I think of the two countries as being like siblings, very different from each other, frequently annoyed with each other, differing on nearly everything, sometimes not even on speaking terms --but siblings nevertheless, there for each other when needed. It is quite likely that neither would have won its revolution and become, together, the two oldest democracies in the world without the help of the other.

She sits in Gothic splendor on the Quai, overlooking the Seine and much of what is most beautiful about Paris, like the Grande Dame she is. No longer young, she could be overcome by memories, having witnessed and participated in so much history for so long—the birth of two democracies, two of the planet's most terrible wars, one of its most fascinating romances—but she is far too involved in modern life to spend much time on that kind of thing. She is a deep well of knowledge, a repository for the lessons of history, a force still today in the lives of people of more than 35 nationalities, all races and backgrounds. Those feeling lost in a country not their own still look to her for spiritual sustenance and guidance, fellowship, food, and love.

I discovered this amazing lady in the mid-seventies, when my husband and I had just been transferred to Paris, after eight years in Latin America , and I attended the three and 1 /2 day orientation program called "Bloom Where You Are Planted," and knew I would be back to experience more of The Lady's magic.

I would walk in on a Sunday morning during our three years in Paris and be hit with glorious music, breathtaking architecture, centuries of history, a brilliant sermon, and fascinating people from all over the world. And of course, that famous Parisian light shining through magnificent stained glass windows.

She is housed, as she has been since 1929, in a magnificent Gothic-style building in Paris' lovely 7th arrondisement, overlooking the Seine, in full view of the Eiffel Tower, at 65 Quai D'Orsay. On a lovely recent fall day, I was last privileged to share the company of this great lady, during a walk along the river, past her front door and the Ponts and Mr. Eiffel's steel gridwork to heaven, which might just be the most beautiful urban walk in the world. Her roots precede this beautiful building, but even in humbler abodes she influenced and participated in history, associating as she did with the likes of Ben Franklin, John Paul Jones, Antoine-Augustin Parmentier and so many others. Those historic roots mingled with other, more literal roots—those of the tobacco plant and the potato when they were first introduced to Europe—there is a reason why a nearby cross street is called Rue Nicot,, why the French, and the rest of us whenever possible, still enjoy a cup of delicious Potage Parmentier (potato soup)—and the soil she sits on is to this day nourished by the bones of French Huguenot martyrs ordered murdered, by the thousands, during the infamous St. Bartholomew's Day Massacre, in August of 1572 with their bodies thrown into a mass grave on the land now occupied by The Lady herself. Hallowed ground indeed.

I think of the church on the left bank of the Seine as "she" because, in the midst of chic, intellectual Paris, which may welcome you once you know the rules, she was there, with open arms, welcoming newbies and residents alike; when we joined the church in 1977, some of the older members remembered The Duke and Duchess of Windsor seeking, and finding, warmth and acceptance while the rest of the world shunned them.

The American Church in Paris is the oldest physical presence of the United States beyond its own borders. It is also the only church ever to have received the Silver Medal of the City of Paris, given in 1972 in recognition of its service to the community. And it was chosen by the French government, in a surprise move on short notice, to be the scene of a massive service of unity with Americans shortly after the terrorist attacks of Sept. 11, 2001.

The church was first officially sanctioned by Napoleon in 1814, and the first sanctuary was built in 1857; at that stage it was an interdenominational fellowship for those adhering to the historic Christian Protestant tradition, and served English speaking expats from the United States and other English speaking countries. The present site is itself so loaded with history, of Protestantism in France and other cultural phenomenon, that I like to think the church is nourished by these other roots as well.

Like Paris itself, she is a mix of the magnificent and the tragic, man-kind's basest impulses and its best. When she is not remembering the great events of history she has witnessed, she sometimes communes with her ancestors. Until recent times there stood, just behind the site, a tavern called The Auberge of the Swan, originally constructed as a hunting lodge for Henry IV. Later the tavern was much frequented by Ben Franklin and Beaumarchaise. One evening the two dined there with a young naval officer named John Paul (who later changed his name to John Paul Jones to avoid capture by the British Navy and hanging for the crime of piracy) and around the table plans were com-pleted for the French government to purchase a Dutch vessel, to be commanded by Captain Jones and to be used to harass the British coast. The vessel was, of course, The Bonhomme Richard, and John Paul Jones became the Father of the American Navy--but that is an-other story, already well told in the history books.

So much of the history of Protestantism in France is shadowed by an ancient French mistrust of the faith, epitomized by the aforementioned Saint Bartholomew's Day massacre, a targeted group of assassinations, followed by a Roman Catholic wave of mob violence. The massacre began two days after the attempted assassination of Admiral Gaspard de Coligny, the military and political leader of the Huguenots. Starting on Aug. 23, 1572 (the eve of the feast of Bartholomew the Apostle) the new king ordered the murders of a group of Huguenot leaders, in Paris for the wedding of the Protestant Margaret of Navarre to Catherine of Medici's Catholic son Henry, an alliance that was supposed to bring unity and reconciliation.

The violence spread throughout Paris, then other parts of France, and ultimately resulted in the deaths of anywhere from 5,000 to the 70,000 reported by the contemporary Huguenot duc de Sully, who himself barely escaped death. The bodies of the dead were collected in carts and thrown into the Seine, whose waters turned red with blood, but were later retrieved and buried on what is now the site of The American Church in Paris.

But what, you ask, about the tobacco, and the potato?

The Rue Nicot still leads from the heart of the Seventh Arrondisement to the Quai D'Orsay, in honor of a young French Ambassador, Jean Nicot, sent by his government to Portugal to negotiate the marriage of six-year-old Princess Marguerite de Valois to five-year-old King Sebastian of Portugal. When Nicot returned to France he brought tobacco from the New World and introduced snuff to the French Court. The Queen Mother, Catherine de Medici (yes, her again) became an instant tobacco convert. More and more of the fashionable people of Paris began to use the plant, making Nicot a celebrity. The tobacco plant, Nicotiana, is named after him, as is nicotine. Ultimately, he established his tobacco warehouse, on the site where The American Church in Paris now stands.

And potatoes? In a field at the current site of the church, Antoine-Augustin Parmentier planted his first potato field. Potatoes were then regarded as something to be fed only to pigs, and Parmentier was determined to prove otherwise, to prove in fact that this nutritious and easily cultivated vegetable would be the answer to France's recurring hunger problems in the 18th century. In order to introduce the tubers to Parisian society, he gave a few sacks to a book seller at the Place St. Michel, who gave potatoes away with each sale. Early efforts were unsuccessful, as potatoes had long been considered unhealthy for humans. Parmentier was redeemed, however, and his fortune secured, when mass starvation during the Famine of 1785 was avoided because of Parmentier's many soup kitchens in Paris, deploying rich, steaming potato soup into the hands of the starving masses. But first, he had conducted a well-oiled campaign to bring the humble root to the attention of the Royals, presenting a potato flower to Louis XVI, who reputedly popped it into his buttonhole, while Marie Antoinette se-cured a bouquet in her bosom. Then he sent potatoes into genteel soci-ety, staging elaborate 5 and 6 course potato dinners for the movers and shakers of the day, including America's charming new diplomat, Ben Franklin, who, among others was invited to a dinner at his apartment at which every dish, from the opening now-famous Potage Parmentier to the coffee and after-dinner liquor, was made with potatoes.

Parmentier's potato fields had American backing, as did the company founded by Jean Nicot, who established his tobacco warehouse on the current site, originally a small island called "L'ile du Cygne," or Swan Island, which extended from the Pont des Invalides to the Pont de l'Alma. The site has been filled in and is no longer an island. The now ubiquitous steak et frites probably indicate that Parmentier was successful.

The music program has always been among the many pleasures of at-tendance at The American Church in Paris. When we arrived in 1978, it was under the direction of a newly hired tall, thin young man named Fred Gramman. Today he is still the director of a much expanded and justly renowned program which includes multiple handbell choirs, a fantastic organ and several choirs. Fred is still tall and thin and looks much as he did all those years ago, with perhaps just a few grey hairs thrown into the mix. And his life, along with the equipment and con-tent of the music program, has greatly expanded and improved during those decades. He recalls arriving in Paris with his wife, both young music students, and living in a fifth floor walk up without heat or air conditioning. It was heated with a wood burning stove, the wood, of course, carried up all those flights of stairs by Mr. Gramman himself. Some nights, he says, they were so cold that they brought his wife's hair dryer into bed with them--running, of course.

There was no written music available when Mr. Gramman took the job; there is now a massive library. There was just one one-octave set of handbells (a particular passion of Gramman's). There are now four sets with many octaves, including English, Dutch and White Chapel, to outfit two adult choirs and a youth choir. His dream is to one day have a carillon in the tower, which won't support a free-swinging bell. With its price tag of $250,000, it is a dream that may have to be deferred. Along with the music library, the organ, and the handbells, his living conditions are also, he reports, much better.

The original English-speaking congregation, lacking facilities of its own, met in the Oratoire on the Rue de Rivoli in space generously provided for them by their French counterparts, and more than 100 years later, when the German occupation during World War II forced the evacuation of the American minister, then Dr. Clayton Williams, a French minister performed services for a handful of elderly American and British residents too old for either evacuation or concentration camps. During that period the Rev. Andre Monod, then more than 60 years old, walked the nearly 30 miles round trip from St. Germain-en-laye, in the absence of trains, buses or cars, that services might continue. Prayers for the President of the United States were offered in the church each Sunday of the Occupation. French people frequently attended to show silent support and to receive news. When Dr. Williams was one of six Americans to return to France after the war he brought carloads of relief supplies.

Napoleon III was so impressed by the religious freedom of the United States that he turned four churches over to the Protestants, one being the Oratoire on the Rue de Rivoli, where for the first time the small American congregation was able to gather in a public place. In 1857 the Americans were allowed to build their own church at 21 Rue de Berri, later home for some years to The International Herald Tribune (now The New York Times International Tribune), with the stipulation that services be conducted solely in English. From the beginning the congregation's emphasis, for the first time in the history of Protestantism, was on nondenominationalism, and from then until now it's doors and facilities have been open to all.

Four U.S. presidents, Ulysses S. Grant, Theodore Roosevelt, Woodrow Wilson and Ronald Reagan attended services in the church, and one long-time member recalled a boyish Edward Kennedy, future presidential candidate, enjoying the Sunday dances as a young bachelor in Paris. Dr. Martin Luther King Jr. preached there while in Europe to accept his Nobel prize.

The present building, a 15th-century-Gothic-style structure containing Louis Comfort Tiffany stained glass windows considered to be the finest modern glass in Europe, and a five-floor English Gothic church house, was built in 1929 at a cost of one million dollars. That the church did not have to go into debt to finance this enormous undertaking reflects the fact that many of the Americans living in Paris at that time were long-term wealthy residents able to be generous to their church. The wonderful windows, for example, hand-made in Tiffany's studio in New York, cost $2,500 when they were purchased by Rodman Wannamaker of Philadelphia and donated to the church.

A Festival of the Arts was begun in the 1930's to raise money for renovation and restoration. Such personages as The Duchess of Windsor and Eleanor Roosevelt cut the ribbon to open those events. One wonders if they met, and if so, what they had to say to each other. The Duke and Duchess had originally asked to be married in The American Church in Paris, but were turned down because neither the American nor the French officials involved wished to risk alienating an important ally with war almost certainly just around the corner.

All eyes, of course, were on the controversial duchess when she entered, wearing her soon-to-become famous Cartier jewels. She was heard to

mutter that "the King should have been seated first." And her outfit-
-Mainbocher? Dior? Vionnet? Imagine the contrast between her and
the plain-spoken, plainly dressed Mrs. Roosevelt, the one all style and
little substance, the other all substance and little style. Most likely in a
simple but well-cut grey suit, the ever-present hat and sensible shoes.

Always at the forefront of change and current events, The American
Church in Paris remains a beacon for newcomers and long-time English
speaking residents. In 1976 the three day program called "Bloom
Where You are Planted" was established and is to this day the gold
standard for cross-cultural training and international settling in. The
huge church is filled every October with English-speaking newcomers
from all over the world who are greeted by vendors selling practically
every product and service you might need during your stay, and speak-
ers on everything from French food and cooking, French traffic laws
(and how to survive the torture of trying to get a license to drive), social
customs, manners, architecture, history, and pretty much anything else
you might care to ask about. At the end of three days, you will have
learned much of what you need to know about living there, and met
the people who are likely to become your friends throughout your stay,
and perhaps forever.

The current pastor, Dr. Scott Herr, tells me how different things are
today from when we were members in the 1970's and the majority of
the mostly American and British congregants were, if not fabulously
wealthy, at least affluent members of the international arts, business
and academic community, able to support their church. Today the
church serves people from nearly 50 nations and 35 denominations,
many of them poor, many of them refugees.

Serving the underserved brings the church closer to the mandate from
Jesus, but the paucity of large donations from wealthy patrons, or
even smaller donations from less affluent members, makes for a great

challenge. Every language is spoken although services are still in English, and it remains at its heart an American away from home, as witnessed by its introduction of Boy and Girl Scouting, Alcoholics Anonymous, Weight Watchers, and other such Americanisms to France. Certain dreams, such as for a carillon tower to complement its famed handbell choirs, will probably remain unfulfilled for a while. The remarkable Tiffany windows are in need of repair.

The catacombs beneath the building are still there, housing the youth programs. During the 60's a coffee house there hosted such luminaries as Bob Dylan, Father Berrigan and others. "I love the history, but I'm excited about our future," says Dr. Herr. "We are a taste of the future, a vision of what the world and community can be."

We Americans and the French achieved our democracies within a few short decades of each other, with theirs inspired by ours, each with the help of the other, developing ties that have bound us together through the centuries. Despite deep differences in politics, philosophy, religion, culture and language, we are more alike than different. I never forget the astounding statistic that more French soldiers died at the decisive Battle of Yorktown during the American Revolution than Americans (although technically there were no Americans then, only colonists). And the French remember American sacrifices on their behalf whenever they visit the heart-breaking cemeteries of Normandy, Brittany and Lorraine.

And so this amazing lady, and her amazing congregation within, sits there still, on one of the most beautiful streets in the world, overlooking the Seine, enriched by the blood of martyrs, the gifts of the wealthy, the aspirations and diversity of the poor and persecuted, comfortable with her past, facing the future unafraid, welcoming all who seek a spiritual home away from home.

Chapter 7

———— ❧ ————

THE HALF-WAY HOUSE PRISON BLUES

SOMETIMES IT WAS easy to tell how a life had gone so wrong. "I was born in a prison and so was my mother," one would say. Or from another: "I don't mind being in prison. This is the first time in my life I've had a roof over my head, three meals a day, and a place to sleep at night." Or this: "This is no big deal. Everyone goes to prison at some point. I'm only doing six months this time; I didn't even bother to tell anyone I'd be away."

Other times it was harder. Martha was young, in her 30's I'd guess, attractive, well-spoken, intelligent, from what sounded like a conventional middle-class background. But she'd married the wrong guy. His illegal drugs were found in their refrigerator, thus making her an accomplice to a crime. Under mandatory sentencing laws, this mother of two young children got 10 years in prison. She always arrived at our meeting room in the half-way house first, holding two cups of hot fresh coffee, one for herself and the other, fixed just the way I liked it, for me.

She was transitioning out when I met her. She was one of those who turned up for my journaling class, and one of the few who stayed. Her dream, she said, was to first get a divorce from the guy who had landed her there, then buy a truck outfitted for painting and wallpapering work. But she wondered if anyone would ever hire her with her record. She was amazed and thrilled when I said that I certainly would, I was always looking for help like that.

The rules said that any course offered in the half-way house had to be open to all inmates, although none had to participate if they didn't want to. Thirty or more had turned up for the first meeting, mostly out of curiosity, and for something new to do (it gets pretty boring in there), down to maybe 15 at the next. Now we were down to the six who would remain and become my group. The motivated ones. The ones who got it, the ones who might get out and stay out.

I sympathized with those who'd dropped out. It's not easy to venture into strange territory, for which you know you're completely unprepared. Just driving in had made me uneasy. I'd submitted to the CORI criminal back ground check, turned in my driver's license, agreed to never reveal my last name or address—but as one inmate said, "Hey, if we really wanted to find out where you live, we could. Your car is parked right in the yard and we all know how to run a license check…" I didn't even know if that was true, but it did nothing to steady my nerves.

Looking around at the wary yet hopeful faces of women who knew they needed to make changes, but didn't yet know how or what, I was glad to be there, to offer help in whatever way I could. I couldn't change their lives for them, but perhaps I could help them gain enough confidence and self-esteem to do it themselves. I had had to go through my own educational journey, learning more about the prison system and, in particular, women in prison, just to be there. And it had made me sympathetic to their plight. I hadn't known, for example, that 95 percent of all prison inmates are male, only 5 percent are female. Of the 95 percent who are male, 95 percent of those are in for crimes of violence, and thus will be there for a long time. Among women inmates, 95 percent are there for rather petty non-violent crimes and misdemeanors, and thus have much shorter sentences, usually months, occasionally years, as opposed to years and decades.

So resources for job training, psychological counseling, addiction treatment, and even better physical facilities go to the men, in the hope that if and when they do get out, they will be prepared for a different kind of life and will not return. For the women, however, there is neither time nor money for any of that. And because they are generally from chaotic families, with little education, they go back to the same "survival crimes," i.e. prostitution, small-time drug dealing, etc. that brought them there in the first place, leading to a wasteful (of lives as well as money) and expensive recidivism rate. My class fell under the umbrella of a broader range of services designed to bring that rate down. Statistics proved that it worked.

This terrible disparity had been true from the beginning, when women were imprisoned, for indeterminate lengths of time for such "crimes" as "stubbornness," drunkenness, homelessness, disobedience. It had begun with the witch trials, relics and aspects of which continued on for hundreds of years.

MCI (Massachusetts Correctional Institution) Framingham, the country's oldest prison for women, has a long and checkered history, veering throughout the centuries from the most enlightened and humane of places to among the worst and most punitive. When Civil War General Bery Butter became governor of Massachusetts in 1883, he asked Clara Barton, founder of the American Red Cross, to become the third superintendent at what was then called "Reformation Prison for Women at Sherborn, MA." Barton was from a family that had settled in New England in the 16th century; she was a descendant of Salem "witches," several of whom had been hung, but one of whom escaped to found Salem End, a colony in Framingham, in 1693. She had deep roots as an American, as a rebel, and as a humanist. She found a population in Framingham that had been arrested and confined, sometimes "indefinitely," for such crimes as "stubbornness, drunkenness, homelessness, lewdness, cohabitation, being criminally intimate with men, disobedience."

She established a system based on humane care, including mental and physical health services, educational opportunities, job training, and respect for each individual. Others have tried hard to continue and improve on such policies, but eventually "tough on crime" politicians, usually with support from the voting public which doesn't want its tax dollars "squandered" on "coddling criminals," prevail.

Sixty five percent of inmates have mental health issues. Most were abused, sexually or otherwise, as children, making it three times the rate of male inmates.

But back to our group:

We had few rules. Just show up and bring some writing to share. If there were things you needed to write about for therapeutic reasons but didn't care to share, that was fine, but you needed to bring something, however short, that could be shared.

Marvella was resistant. She came several times, clutching some handwritten pages, but refusing to read them. Ultimately I realized that she, and several others, were embarrassed by their lack of education, their poor spelling and grammar, their inability to put a sentence together. Some were embarrassed to write about their lives, their only material, because they were so barren, because there was nothing they could take pride in, including, perhaps especially, their own parents. I explained that I didn't care about any of that, this was not school, we all had something of value to share.

Watching them slowly, over the weeks and years, open up, own their own lives and tell their stories, was like watching flowers bloom, with themselves as the gardeners. They learned to separate the weeds from the productive plants, to water and fertilize where needed, to remove weaker plants and reduce crowding if necessary and to take pride in themselves. The resulting writing was beautiful and moving.

Annette: "I wanted to be a Girl Scout so bad when I was a kid. My mother laughed so hard at the idea of someone like me being a Girl Scout. "Oh Lord," she'd say, the giggles bubbling up. "I can see it now. You—a Girl Scout." I didn't normally give grades, that wasn't what this group was about, but I put an A+ on her piece. Her pride and happiness put a glow on my face too, one that lasts to this day when I think about it.

As one of the teachers, I was part of a mentoring program in which a mentor was paired with an inmate. As such I could attend various programs on subjects relevant to my work, such as The Addictive Personality, recovery work, etc. At one such program, attended by both inmates and mentors, we were all asked to take a simplified version of a personality test which, in the end would reveal whether we were basically Passive or Aggressive types. Then we were asked to raise our hands to indicate into which group we fell.

I was positive the inmates would all be Aggressives, breaking rules and maybe store windows, while we "good girls" would be the Passives. I couldn't have been more wrong. Every inmate raised her hand when Passives were asked to identify, and every mentor the same when

Aggressives were called upon. How could this be? Turns out Passives, those with low self-esteem, did as they were told. If husband or boyfriend said, "I'm storing drugs in our refrigerator," so it was. If Mom said, "Go out and hustle so you can get me some drugs," ditto. We Aggressives, on the other hand, would have told them all where to go. Guess who landed in prison?

The holiday season, with its emphasis on family reunions, joy and happiness, children's glowing faces, wonderful food, tended to be a difficult and depressing time for these women who had so little of such things, and sadness could settle over the grim building like a shroud. Some had lost their children forever. Others saw theirs on occasional visits, but felt they had little to offer them. Some looked forward to regaining theirs when they got out, but would not be seeing them for the holidays.

We all decided that our weekly sessions would continue and we would try to make the season as festive as possible by throwing ourselves a little party. I volunteered to seek permission to bring in food and party supplies but they wouldn't hear of it. They would do everything and I would be their guest. Because it was to be held at 3 PM, I was assuming a tea and cookies kind of thing.

Meanwhile, another group of which I was a member began planning its annual Christmas lunch at noon of that same day. No problem, I thought, I'll have lunch with them, then head over to my writing group for coffee and dessert, or tea and cookies, whatever.

Lunch was huge, delicious, filling. "Oh no," I thought. "I can't eat again. Well, I'll just tell them I'm on a diet or something, and enjoy coffee with them." When I walked into our meeting room, it was obvious the women had gone to a lot of trouble—the dreary prison-issue beige room where we met had been transformed into a fairyland with imaginative and beautiful hand-made decorations. And the wonderful smells wafting from the nearby kitchenette were not speaking of store-bought cookies.

With limited (read: no) resources, using the pennies they earned at their prison "jobs," and salvaged canned goods, contraband, and whatever else they could get their hands on, they had made fabulous Spanish rice, salads, made-from-scratch bread, desserts of every description (flan, rice pudding, cake—you name it). Their faces were no longer depressed, at least for the day; they were filled with pride of accomplishment at having pulled off such a magnificent surprise, much welcoming love and, yes—holiday spirit.

After a weak protest about my "diet," which was immediately booed down, I made some quick mental calculations. Yes, I was already stuffed to the gills and the thought of any more food, much less the heavy spread before me, made me almost sick. But I also saw how important this was to them, how much time, effort and sacrifice had gone into it, and I knew what I had to do.

I put a big smile on my face, told them I was nearly starving to death, and sat down to one of the most memorable meals of my life.

Postscript: Framingham has, throughout its long history, alternated between being one of the most miserable of black holes to fall into, and one of the most modern and humane places of reform and hope for those who had lost hope. To learn more about Framingham, and thus our prison system in general, I recommend "A World Apart, Women, Prison, and Life Behind Bars, by Cristina Rathbone, available on

Amazon. With compassion, precision, persistence and great patience, she has told the full story of several women behind bars, the forces that put them there, the conditions they endure, and their hopes for the future, for themselves and their children.

Chapter 8

JENNIE

JENNIE MEETS THE HEMINGWAYS

THE YEAR WAS 1909, and the country was experiencing its worst recession in 100 years. But Jennie was feeling buoyant; no recession could be worse than the depression she felt at the thought of continuing to teach in a one room school in her small, rural, dusty northern Illinois home town of Maple Park, Illinois. And the ad in The Chicago Tribune, when it perhaps really was, as claimed, the World's Greatest Newspaper, was enticing. The Tribune was a Midwestern institution, having boldly championed abolition before the idea had many followers. Its strong support of Abraham Lincoln when so many others were still calling him "the big black ape from the backwoods" had helped to elect our greatest president. As the daughter of a Civil War veteran (on the Union side, of course), the word of the biggest newspaper in Illinois, The Land of Lincoln, carried weight with Jennie and every one she knew.

Strong and fearless though she was, doubts assailed her when she stood at the door of that most imposing of institutions, Oak Park Hospital. The only thing posh, sprawling sophisticated Oak Park had in common with Maple Park, where she had lived her entire life, was that they were both named for trees. She had earned a teaching certificate from Illinois State College in 1908, at a time when most of her peers graduated only from the eighth grade, had taught for a year but had not liked it, and decided to try nursing, one of the few other careers newly open to women.

"Are my clothes good enough?" she wondered. She had dressed with care in her very best--a white, lace-trimmed blouse with long, full sleeves, a long narrow navy blue skirt, all accented with a gold bracelet, a gold necklace, and a cameo brooch centered on the high lace collar. Cobalt blue eyes gazed in wonder at the impressive surroundings. Long thick chestnut-colored hair was piled high atop her head. "Oh no, my hair" she thought in panic. It had looked fine when she had begun her train ride earlier in the day, but now....? It must have passed muster, because she was greeted at the door and ushered to the nurses' cottage where she would be expected to live for the next three years. She was 30 years old. Her arrival at this newly-opened institution, part of the nation-wide movement to build hospitals and professionalize medical care, which had previously been entrusted to untrained family members and adminis-tered at home, had been by a circuitous route. She had begun her studies at West Side Hospital, Chicago, but had been shocked, on the first day, to find her bed full of bedbugs. She and another student nurse were given cleaning supplies with which to scrub away the problem, and they spent the rest of the day trying to do just that. The following day the little devils were back "in full force," as she later recalled.

She applied for an immediate transfer to the newly-opened, much more luxurious Oak Park School of Nursing. True to form, it was lead by a reknowned and charismatic physician in order to attract attention, stu-dents and funding. In this case, Dr. Clarence Hemingway filled this role.

No copy of that Tribune ad exists, but here is what Oak Leaves, the newspaper of record in Oak Park, Ill, had to say in February of 1907: Arrangements have been completed for the course of instruction...in the Oak Park Hospital Training School for Nurses. Applicants must be over 20 years of age and under 30 years. Applicants for advanced standing can only be received upon examination for a period of not less than one year. Applicants must present certificates of good moral character...during the first year courses in nursing, anatomy, and physiology, cooking and dietetics, chemistry and materia medica will be given...to furnish a foundation for...Lectures on pathology, medicine, surgery and obstetrics the second year. In addition to these, brief courses in bacteriology, anatomy, urinalysis, and toxicology...in the third year lectures on eye, ear, nose and throat, children's diseases...ethics of nursing...

Not for the faint of heart, but Jennie was never that. The fifth of nine children, her mother had died when she was seven. Her father, the aforementioned civil war veteran, farmed the 40 acres he had received as pay for his service, but proceeded to marry three more times, in fairly rapid succession, leaving little time or money to help or guide Jennie or her siblings. She had been on her own for a long time, and had succeeded in earning her teaching certificate at Illinois State College (now Northern Illinois University) in 1908, at a time when most of her peers graduated only from the eighth grade. She had taught school for a year but did not enjoy it. Maybe nursing, another of the few careers open to women at that time, would be better.

She was determined to be a member of that first nursing class at Oak Park Hospital.

Courses were to be taught, not only by nursing staff, but by the renowned Dr. Clarence Hemingway himself, one of the most distinguished doctors in the greater Chicago area and husband of equally renowned Grace Hall Hemingway, opera singer, artist, teacher and socialite. They were well known, not only for their professional accomplishments but for their beautiful homes, stunning family, and impressive pedigree. No wonder Jennie worried whether her clothes and hair measured up!

Jennie excelled in school and caught the attention of Dr. Hemingway, who asked her to do some private nursing in his home when his wife was ill. Most doctors kept their office in their home at that time, and Dr. Hemingway was no exception. At that point four of their eventual six children had been born, including their third child, the one day to become famous Ernest, then ten years old. As her professional interests were far more interesting to her than running a home, Mrs. Hemingway always maintained a large, live-in staff, including cooks, nannies, maids, gardeners. A busy place indeed.

But all was not well in paradise, as it so frequently isn't. It was not only the country that was in a depression; there were already small but visible cracks in the foundations of this magnificent edifice that was the Hemingway family. Clarence, in particular, was dealing with a recurring, but this time more severe depression of his own. Despite the appearance of great wealth, he was dealing with intense financial pressures, brought on by the very need to maintain the appearance of wealth in that wealth-conscious society. And there were marital pressures. Although the Hemingways owned, and frequently used, a Michigan lake cottage for summer vacations, Grace was threatening to buy a cottage of her own across the lake, perhaps to escape the noise and tensions of her ever-growing family; and according to gossip she would be sharing it with a female student. She was planning to pay for it with her inheritance, but of course Dr. Hemingway could think of better uses for that money. Only much later would Jennie, and the rest of the world, learn that alcoholism, mental illness and suicide ran through that family like boll weevils though a cotton field. In 1928, upon receiving a diagnosis of diabetes, already ill with heart disease Dr. Hemingway, would kill himself with a Civil War era "Long John" revolver, inherited from his father, at age 58. He was found by his son Leicester, who would do the same in

1982. Ernest, by then a world-renowned writer, would mimic this act, at the same age. Of the six Hemingway siblings, three would eventually take their own lives.

The writer John Dos Passos, Ernest's great friend in later life, said he had never met a man who hated his mother as much as Ernest hated his. And Martha Gelhorn, Hemingway's third wife, said "He (Ernest) hated his mother, with reason. She was solid hell, a big, false, lying woman. Everything about her was virtuous and untrue…no woman should ever marry a man who hates his mother." Clarence apparently had many reasons to be depressed.

It was into this atmosphere that Jennie would bring her cobalt eyes, her calm demeanor, her ability to stay cool in a crisis, and her sparkling Irish wit like a breath of fresh country air. Family lore tells us that Dr. Hemingway chose Jennie to be his personal nurse, helping care for Grace and the children during times of illness.

Jennie was no stranger to hardship, grief, financial insecurity, family turmoil. The fifth of nine children, she was seven years old when her mother died in childbirth, leaving Jennie and her siblings to fend for themselves while caring for the newborn. Her father, of whom she never spoke because, she said, "I wasn't proud of him," remarried three times; there were two divorces, unheard of at that time in their small mostly Catholic town. She never spoke a word, throughout her long life, about these "stepmothers." Accustomed to dealing with life's difficulties, and difficult people, Jennie would bring the same grace and inborn elegance to the Hemingway household that she had brought to her own.

But bad luck struck—in April, near the end of her first year, she became ill with diphtheria, which left her legs paralysed. She went home to recover, eventually regaining use of her legs, but never regained her full level of energy. She returned to school the following September, but realized she was too far behind to catch up.

She returned to DeKalb, a larger town near Maple Park, to work as a nurse at DeKalb hospital, to marry and raise her family, and to serve as matriarch and role model to an ever-expanding clan. She had enjoyed Oak Park, but she was a country girl at heart. She missed her sisters and the undulating fields of golden corn and wheat.

Jennie

PASSPORT TO THE WORLD

Loving Frank

Much as she loved to dance and go out, sociable being that she was, Jennie had not been all that excited about attending the dance that cold Saturday evening. It would be fun, of course, or at least more fun than staying home—it would include plenty of all the things she liked best: friends, family, food, music, dancing. She would be going with her boyfriend Jim, dear old reliable Jim, who would pick her up in his creaky carriage, pulled by a team of ancient but dependable horses. Jim wasn't much of a dancer—but he tried. And Jim, it had often been pointed out to her, was a Democrat and a Catholic, like herself—the perfect match for a woman of 34 who wanted marriage and children. Or so she had been told.

She looked around the familiar house where the dance was about to begin. The fiddler was just warming up his instrument, the hot mulled cider was being poured—when suddenly the door opened and a well-dressed, handsome man rushed in, bringing the cold air with him. Why the rush? Well, that's just the way Frank Klein was—even his spirited team of horses were stomping their feet impatiently. Everyone turned to look; most already knew this young farmer who was also the road commissioner, and active in local Republican politics. Though not religious himself, he had been raised in a Protestant home—thus making him totally unsuitable for Jennie. She noted the intoxicating scent of Bay Rum cologne that followed him. Later she would remember the undertones of alcohol and tobacco, even more dangerously intoxicating. And later she would think she should have paid more attention to those undertones. Handsome and charming young men who could "hold their liquor" frequently turn into mean, abusive drunks as they age—and Frank did.

"Care to dance?" he asked, his brown eyes as intense as her blue. "Why yes," she replied without hesitation.

Faithful Jim looked on, puzzled and unhappy. Jim wasn't bad-looking—but Frank was handsome! Jim was reliable and loving—Frank was dashing. Her time in the city had awakened a taste for excitement, drama, the unknown.

After a few months of back and forthing—Frank would come courting and Jim would be there, so Frank would storm off—or vice versa—or Jim would send a box of chocolates and Frank would send a bigger box, Frank finally proposed and Jennie accepted. She apparently failed to notice that he came with what must have seemed like a swarm of unmarried jealous sisters, used to having their brother to themselves, and, worse, an invalid aunt who lived with Frank, and presided over the family home in which Jennie would live, who would need years of intense nursing care, which Jennie would provide, despite her years of mistreatment at the hands of this woman.

"Why?" she was sometimes asked. "Well, he had the best team of horses in the county!" she would reply. So easy to be blind to even the most important things when you are in love.

They were married in January of 1913; the first of their six children, Frank Theodore Jr., was born in December of that year. Twin girls who died in infancy soon followed, survived by another son and two daughters. Perhaps they were saved from the deadly fate of so many infants of that era by the nursing skills of their mother. Jennie was 36 when her oldest child was born, 43 when her youngest arrived.

JENNIE AND HER HOBOS

Jennie's reputation for generosity, steadiness, kindness and calm DURING the storm came, perhaps, to fullest flower during The Great Depression. After all, she had been through such times before and had known much grief since her Oak Park adventure into the larger world. Her two lost girls were the hardest; more than 40 years later, with tears pouring down her face (the only time I ever saw her cry) she would talk about her two "beautiful girls."

Jennie devoted her life to her remaining children, and eventually grandchildren, and by using her nursing skills to serve her community, delivering babies (there are tales of delivering babies in the middle of winter in drafty, poorly heated farmhouses in the midst of a brutal upper Midwestern winter and warming the wrapped newborn on the still-warm open door of a pre-heated oven.) When asked by a reporter on her 100th birthday what had been the greatest medical advance during her nursing years she replied, "aspirin." I picture her distributing it lavishly, diminishing physical pain with pills, emotional pain with her ability to listen intently and gifting the patient with those never-wavering cobalt eyes.

But she had gifts for others too, those often shunned by society. It was the Depression, and homeless, unemployed men roamed the countryside, hopping trains when they could, seeking a day's work for a day's pay at farms, sleeping in hidden hobo jungles. There were so many of them, and the Depression lasted so long, that they formed their own culture, community, communication system, songs, and recipes for campfire dinners (although mostly each one just threw into the communal pot left over from the previous tenants what he had—don't ask.) They developed their own sign language, leaving carved symbols on trees, lampposts, mailboxes with directions for the nearest jungle (just out of the way places in wooded areas where they would not be seen and thrown out). Those signs left at farms might warn the next one to keep going, the farmer here had a gun and would use it, or a vicious dog might attack, or other indications of the prevailing hostility towards, and fear of the hobos.

There were also marks indicating that this was a friendly place where you might find a day's work, for pay, and/or a barn to sleep in, perhaps even a hot, home-cooked meal. The latter sign was on a tree at the end of Jennie's driveway. Knowing her personality, compassion, friendliness, curiosity, warmth, I enjoy imagining one of her encounters with a hobo.

OLD RUST

Old Rust hesitated, then looked again at the wrinkled "map" in his wrinkled hand. Yep, that old farmhouse should be coming right up.

And, suddenly, there it was, set quite far back from the road, faded white in a nearly treeless yard. He looked at the mailbox. Yes, it was there, a discreet mark carved into its post indicating that this was a place where he might be given a meal and perhaps more.

"The sign of the hobo," they called it, during the dark days of The Great Depression. Other signs on his map indicated the location of the nearest "hobo jungle", perhaps, where hobos congregated to make a "mulligan stew" and camp out before hitting the road again, then hopping a train to somewhere else, somewhere they might find work. Other signs warned of stingy (or perhaps hungry themselves) people who would slam the door in your face.

He looked at the peeling paint on the house and thought of the days when people like this would have called people like him to come paint it, and he and others like him would have proudly worked for a living. But this place was said to be hospitable.

He knocked on the door. The lady of the house (and she was a lady, despite her shabby surroundings) opened the door and smiled. Cobalt eyes lit up his day. She had seen such ruined men before. "Come in and have dinner," she said. "There are a couple of things I'd like you to do for me while I get it ready, if you are willing." Jennie had a way about her. How like her to know that his dignity required the opportunity to work in return for hospitality.

How long had it been since he'd known the joy of working for his living? How wonderful was it that she had offered food—he was starving--? And Jennie was a wonderful cook.

"Couldn't help but notice the gravestones out there—may I ask?" He thought it only polite to try to make conversation. The beautiful face turned away, revealing a fine Irish profile. "My two infant and toddler twin daughters," she said curtly, and he knew that conversation was over.

"Old Rust" (he was called Joe when he was a working man; the first thing a man lost when he hit the road was his real name, and the first thing he gained was a nickname) put down his coat, rust-colored from too many nights of using it as a mattress when he slept on the ground. The second thing he lost was his individuality. Live as a hobo for long enough and all begin to look alike, from lack of nutrition, lack of personal hygiene, lack of medical care, lack of hope.

He had finished his meal and finished the tasks she had set him to. It was time to move on.

"Goodbye," she said, her smile back in place. "May God go with you." Rust-colored eyes met cobalt blue. Both had known hard times. Rust-colored hands met porcelain white. Both had known hard work.

He looked at his wrinkled map to locate the nearest hobo jungle. As he left he carved a + by the sign already on the mailbox.

Once again he was on his way, whistling this time.

What's in a Name?

We all thought we knew her so well—she had been with us for more than a century, after all—and I had lived with her for three years and six months—but as it turned out, we didn't even know her name. It was Mary Jane, we were always told, and Jennie was her nickname. But then her daughter gave me Jennie's high school diploma many years after her death and there, in beautiful calligraphy on genuine parchment (leather—documents like that were works of art in those days) her name is clearly written—Jennie Magdalene. And then my brother found the yearbook from her year at Northern Illinois State Teachers College where Jane Magdalen is equally as clearly written. What was going on?

With a little sleuthing I realized that most people of her era were born at home; there may or may not have been a birth certificate issued. Your parents gave you a name, but nicknames ensued over the years and the original name could easily get lost, especially if your mother died when you were seven and your father and his subsequent wives took little interest in you. And, devout lifelong Catholic that she was, she would have taken a saint's name at First Communion. Clearly, she chose that of another misunderstood auburn-haired beauty, Mary Magdalene. Thus two Marys were of great significance in her life, Mary the mother of Jesus, to whom she prayed daily with the help of her treasured Rosary, and The Magdalene, whom she chose as her guiding light. This realization inspired me to take a closer look at both.

Jesus' words to John and Mary, his mother, as he was dying on the cross: to John; "Behold your mother." To Mary: "Woman, behold your son." Thus, he entrusted John to spread his message throughout the world, accompanied and helped by his mother, and also to take care of his mother, calling John now her son. But sometimes I wonder—who took care of whom? Their travels together, according to tradition, involved primitive conditions in a wooden sailing ship over rough seas to foreign lands, present day Greece and Turkey in particular, where their message was not always welcomed; the local people had their own gods and goddesses, and silversmiths were getting rich making and selling images of them to the locals and tourists. They were not happy to hear strangers telling their customers about one God only, who forbade graven images.

Magnificent Renaissance art shows us a limpid Virgen, forever holding her child, eyes downcast. I suspect there was a lot more to her than that. She raised a brilliant son and made sure he got the best available education. She traveled with him, listened to him and the disciples as they hammered out the new philosophy, no doubt contributing her own insights. And I'm betting she and the rest of the women (many of whom were financing the whole thing) did most of the heavy lifting when it came to finding, preparing and serving food, making and repairing robes and sandals, etc. Some things never change. And much later, in her travels with John, they must have had many deep conversations, with her contributions feeding his ever-growing thirst for more knowledge and faith. Imagine the hardships endured by a no-longer-young woman in those circumstances. Of course, it is John's name that is on the book; again, some things never change. Yes, I'm sure she was beautiful, kind and gentle, but I'm betting she was also tough as nails. You don't make it into the history books if you're not—and the Bible is a history book.

It is still possible to visit Mary's home in Ephesus, where both John and

Paul preached and where Mary is said to have lived from AD 37 until her death in AD 48. Legend and tradition have always held that Mary lived and taught in Ephesus for several years at the end of her life in a house called Meryemana, discovered in 1891 by Lazarist priests from Smyrna acting on a dream/vision of Catherine Emmerich, a bedridden German nun who had never left her convent, but was able to describe the house in exact detail. John is allegedly buried nearby, under the now-ruined Basilica of St. John. It is to this woman that Jennie prayed aloud (Hail Mary, full of grace...) every day of her adult life, naming each of her children and grandchildren as well as others she loved, during her own later years. Through such close communion, she gained some of the first Mary's strength, endurance, character, faith, and love of family.

And what of the second Mary, the Magdalene, Jennie's chosen inspiration? Maligned and slandered for centuries as a prostitute (after all, what kind of woman would consider herself the intellectual and spiritual equal of all those important men, even traveling and debating with them?), it was only with the discovery, centuries later, of contemporary but unpublished scriptures, that her courage, intellect, devotion, and role as an unheralded disciple were appreciated, along with her beauty. Like Jennie, who by all rights should have remained poverty-stricken and uneducated, but who chose to venture out and find a better life, the Magdalene was not content to live the traditional life of the homebound woman of her day. Red-haired beauties have been known to be like that. When the men had fled in terror, it was the Marys who were there to take the murdered body from the cross, bathe it, dress it in clean linens, and give it a decent burial.

And so—what's in a name? Perhaps everything, perhaps nothing. With the miracle of the internet, I learned that the name on her social security records is, indeed, Mary Jane. As for Jennie, she lived her life as she saw fit, with no need for self-aggrandizement. Just plain Jennie was good enough for her—and for me.

Big Shoes to Fill

I loved driving up the long, winding, tree-lined road to the beautiful stone building on a hill in the woods, but within the little town of Dover, Massachusets, where I was living.. This magnificent former seminary was now home to classes of all kinds, including one on Creative Writing, which I was about to begin. A former journalist, trained in the arts of objectivity, fact-based writing, and "keeping myself out of the story," I was finding it difficult to transition to creative writing, even though I was so far sticking to non-fiction. Perhaps here is where I would find the key to breaking through.

I loved the physical beauty of the place, especially on a warm, clear, sunny Indian Summer day like that first day of class, that No Man's Land that is no longer summer but not quite fall, a moment in which to enjoy a few more of summer's pleasures, and to put off, for just bit longer, the rigors of winter. I love the beauty of nature, on such lavish display in this place, and the man-made beauty of the building, so redolent of talent, history, effort, dedication, study. But I also loved the symbolism of that long, curving road that was the starting point of a journey back to myself. It would be so easy—it has been so easy—to just live as the poem suggests (for I have miles to go before I sleep, and promises to keep…) and do all those perfectly worthwhile, necessary even, daily tasks that will all have to be done again tomorrow, while accomplishing nothing that might live on for another day.

But I am so lucky to live a life in which I do not have to be consumed just by tasks of survival, and so lucky to have a place like this, at the bottom of the long winding road, in which to try, just for a few minutes, to live up to the beauty that is etched in softscape and hardscape, stone walls and arched windows, polished floors and rooms full of books.

That first class was filled with interesting, creative people motivated much as I was; career and family demands were no longer at the forefront, we could try doing some of the things we had always wanted to do. One man was a veteran of the Korean War and was writing his war memoir. An older woman was a peace activist, writing about what inspired her, at her age, to head into the city at night, when she would really rather be sleeping, reading, or watching TV, to hold signs and speak at peace rallies, often in the bitter cold of winter. All were smart people who had lead long and interesting lives, and had much to write about. Wow, I thought, some interesting writing will emerge from this group.

And I was right, but in unexpected ways. Our instructor asked us to write something for the next class, the following week, that we would be willing to read aloud. Any topic, any length.

And, without consulting with each other—none of us had ever met before—we all, myself included, chose the same topic—our grandmothers. Since I was going to become a grandmother myself, for the first time, within a few weeks, it hit me hard that this grandmother business was important, I needed to give it a lot of thought. The consequences for getting it right, or wrong, would be long lasting. I have three magnificent granddaughters now, and I am ever aware, not only of how lucky I am, but of how important is every word and every action. They will be remembered.

Jennie at 100

IN THE BEGINNING....

Male English triplets, surnamed Lakin, came over to fight for their country, which was England, in The War of 1812. One stayed and married a Canadian-English-American girl named Adeline, and Adeline married Michael Ryan, an immigrant from Langford, Ireland, one of four sons of a schoolteacher who would produce a long line of schoolteachers. But life in the U.S. of that time was hard for penniless immigrants, especially if they were Irish. "No Irish need apply" signs were still seen everywhere. With a family to support, Michael did what so many immigrants did—he accepted money to fight for another in The Civil War. Much has been written about the "real" reasons for serving in The Civil War, but I've never heard it mentioned that for some, be they poor immigrants or native-borns, it was just a way, perhaps the only way, to earn a living and acquire a home. Michael went in place of another as a way of earning a living, and returned with enough money to buy 40 acres of land in Maple Park, Ill., where he and Adeline had nine children, of whom Jennie was the fifth.

Adeline died giving birth to the youngest, a boy, leaving the large brood motherless. Jennie was seven at the time., and never forgot her first nursing experience—taking care of her little brother with such complete devotion that she fainted twice, from exhaustion. Her father then married and remarried several times, including two divorces, which had to have been shocking and embarrassing in that little, mostly Catholic country town in that Victorian era. Why the many marriages? Had he been so in love with his first wife that he wanted to replace her as quickly as possible, but none measured up? Was he impossible to live with, due possibly to drink, or perhaps the as yet unnamed but not unknown Post Traumatic Stress Disorder, that they all left him? Was raising nine children a little harder than they had thought? We'll never know; we just know it left Jennie and her siblings to fend for themselves and look out for each other, which they did, quite admirably. All on that little farm paid for with Michael's Civil War earnings. Jennie, late in life, remembered seeing him bury gold in one of the barns; a grandson searched with a metal detector, but it was long gone if it had ever been there.

Who knows how much pain her silence about this period of her life speaks of?

I'm still trying to figure out how she became the powerhouse she was under such circumstances. I know her staunch Catholicism and daily prayers were part of it; the moral standards from which she never deviated were part of it; the sisters who raised her and stayed close in every way to the end were part of it; the love she gave so freely to all was part of it; the intelligence that shone so brightly from those cobalt eyes right up until she died at age 102 was part of it. Put it all together and what you have is—character. You can't buy it, you can't sell it, it is the one thing that is not dimmed by age. At 102, the passing years had only burnished it.

Our current passion for attaching a label to everyone, especially women, is nothing new. She lived through The Gibson Girl, The Flapper, Rosie the Riveter, The Fifties Housewife, The Hippie, The Feminist, The Radical Feminist—none of which could begin to convey the complexity of her life and her effect on others. She had no need to label herself or others, and as for Virtue Signaling—her life did that for her, with no need or thought for further self-agrandizement.

This woman who gave me more lasting and valuable and useful gifts than anyone else never gave me money or things, never took me shopping. Probably the annual Easter basket, full of candy and chocolate bunnies, (which I and her ten other grandchildren plus a few great grandchildren towards the end of her long life) continued to receive until I was nearly 40 years old, were the most valuable things she ever gave me until the day, a few years before her death, when she took her diamond ring off her finger and gave it to me. And I still have that gold bracelet she wore to Oak Park, and the leather-bound "Reference Hand-Book For Nurses," by Amanda K. Beck, that served as textbook for that nursing class. I'm glad I don't have to learn the mass of dense and highly technical material within.

You might think that diamond ring would be my most precious possession, and it was, but in fact I gave it to my daughter for her 21st birthday, in the hope of connecting these two lives that have so changed my life, and she now cherishes the simple gold band with the elegant stone that dazzles quietly, just as Jennie did.. But one of my most important lessons from Jennie was that is it people, not possessions, that are important; I can give up things quite easily; it is people I cannot give up easily.

She didn't know how to hold a grudge or feel sorry for herself, although not because her life was always easy. As noted, she gave me nothing, not being a wealthy woman, except for fun, token gifts at holidays.

Nothing, except unfailingly cheerful hospitality and unconditional love to all who entered her life ("How many people did she give a home to?" I once asked one of her sons. "Oh, I don't know, anyone who needed one," he replied).

Nothing, except; a rich sense of humor—she always made me laugh, and it was so easy to make her laugh; daily prayers for each and every member of her large, extended family, named by name—a habit I have since adopted—endless praise, almost no criticism, and what there was couched in the gentlest of terms.

Nothing, except the gift of making every occasion, especially holidays, seem special because of her good cheer, good humor, and wonderful food. This was true even in her 90s and 100s, when she surely was in pain much of the time, but would never say so.

Nothing, except that chiseled face, like the finest cameo accented with cobalt jewels.

She is the person upon whose example I have consciously tried to model myself, and when I get discouraged about falling so short of that high standard, I remind myself that it may have taken her the entire 102 years to reach that state of grace.

Maybe I just need more time.

ACKNOWLEDGEMENTS

Writing this book has been a long journey through my past, but fortunately one I have not had to make alone. So many people have helped me or accompanied me in so many ways that it is difficult to choose just a few--but the following have been especially instrumental.

My daughter Liz has fine editing skills which have helped to find errors, and to improve certain sentences and even whole paragraphs, in some cases whole stories. And her fine computer skills have saved me from many a near-nervous-breakdown.

My brother Ron is a family record-keeper and repository of so much history, familial and otherwise. His insights, memories, and stores of information have been extremely helpful.

My cousin Richard Klein, another repository of family history.

My dear friend of many years, and fellow journalist and writer Linda Andrews, has been a constant source of encouragement and useful advice about everything from potential titles to marketing ideas. What would I do without her?

I took many writing courses at Boston's outstanding writing center,

Grub Street. The fine teachers there helped me make the transition from journalist to creative non-fiction writer. The members of my several writing groups and book clubs have always challenged me to think, and thus write, more clearly and incisively.

And of course, my Aunt Ruth, for being my aunt and believing in me, and Jennie, for being my grandmother and making everything possible.

"Amazing Grace" and "The Lady on the Seine" were previously published in the literary magazine The MacGuffin.

CPSIA information can be obtained
at www.ICGtesting.com
Printed in the USA
FFHW010119160119
50185655-55137FF

9 781478 799467